Jackson Hole à la Carte

EDITED
BY
JANE T. CAMENZIND

ILLUSTRATED
BY
ELIZA CHRYSTIE

PUBLISHED BY
THE JACKSON HOLE ALLIANCE
FOR RESPONSIBLE PLANNING

This cookbook represents another way in which many people have volunteered their time to help protect Jackson Hole.

The Alliance thanks them all.

Two names must be mentioned for their outstanding contribution. Thank you to Eliza Chrystie for bringing our cookbook to life with her wonderful drawings. And deepest appreciation to Janie Camenzind for seeing this cookbook through from its beginning stages to its publication. Their dedication on this project is a testament to their love of the Jackson Hole valley.

First Edition 1986
First Printing 1986
Second Printing 1987

ISBN 0-9617014-0-4

LCCN 86-81363

Additional copies may be ordered from the address below or by using the order form on the last page.
The Jackson Hole Alliance for Responsible Planning
260 East Broadway
Post Office Box 2728
Jackson, Wyoming 83001

Design by Riddell Advertising & Design, Jackson, Wyoming
Type set in Berkeley Oldstyle
Lithography by Thomson-Shore, Inc. on 60lb. Glatfelter

A WORD ABOUT THE JACKSON HOLE ALLIANCE

Jackson Hole is a beautiful, mountainous valley in northwestern Wyoming located just south of Yellowstone and Grand Teton National Parks. It is known for its breathtaking scenery, vast wilderness, and abundance of wildlife, including the largest elk herd in North America.

In 1979, a group of concerned citizens recognized the need for careful management of Jackson Hole's resources. The Jackson Hole Alliance for Responsible Planning (the Jackson Hole Alliance) was formed for this purpose. The Alliance is now an organization of over 1,000 members, most of whom are residents or landowners in Jackson Hole. As a nonprofit, tax-exempt organization, the Alliance's goals are accomplished with the help of a paid professional staff and over 250 active volunteers. Alliance offices are located at 260 East Broadway in Jackson, Wyoming.

All proceeds from the sale of this cookbook go towards the Alliance's work in promoting responsible land management, informed citizen participation and protection of Jackson Hole's unique scenic, wildlife and recreational resources.

For further information on the Alliance, please write:
The Jackson Hole Alliance for Responsible Planning
Post Office Box 2728
Jackson, Wyoming 83001
(307) 733-9417

Afternoon Clouds

ACKNOWLEDGMENTS

THE COOKBOOK COMMITTEE
Jane T. Camenzind, *Chairperson and Editor*
Eliza Chrystie, *Cover Design and Illustrations*

Helen Buehler
Story Clark
Holly Dill

Adelaide Donnan
Rose Fraser
Barbara Hauge

Lisa Bennett Pierson
Tina Close Scott

We sincerely thank the Jackson Hole Alliance members and friends who contributed their time and talents to this project.

We especially thank those who shared their favorite recipes with us. Hundreds of wonderful recipes were submitted, but there was space in the cookbook for only one hundred and four. We apologize to those whose recipes were not included because of reasons of space or similarity.

CONTRIBUTORS

Allen, Pat
Antonich, Bobbie
Ashley, Edie Bennett
Ashley, Steve
Barbour, Judy
Baudisch, Nancy
Bayer, Candy
Blue, Brent
Boyd, Patti
Branton, Gretel
Breitenbach, Lou
Bruun, Paul
Buckingham, Edna
Buis, Peggy
Burroughs, Diane
Busot, Lisa
Camenzind, Franz
Carlman, Leonard
Carlman, Maryellen
Carresco, Carlene
Carter, Helen
Chrystie, Tom
Clark, Iris
Clayton, Betty
Clendenin-Leeds, Heide
Cleveland, Barbara
Cress, Jane
Daus, Ellen
Dejanikus, Carolyn
Dill, Warren
Donaldson, Rhonda
Donnan, Ted
Dowling, Lavinia
Downs, Debbie
Elder, Sue
Elliott, Syd
Esperti, Lisbeth
Euler, Sue
Fanelli, Marianne
Fitzsimmons, Nancy
Fleming, Linda
Fraser, Robert
Gardner, Betty
Gingery, Elaine
Goodman, Christine
Gridley, Mary
Griggs, Kenneth

Hahn, Jean
Hahn, Mary Ann
Haman, Caryn
Hamlin, Jo
Harlander, Nancy
Harrington, Putzi
Haubert, Sally
Hendricks, Patti
Hibberd, Debbie
Hiller, Jackie
Hirschfield, Berte
Hirschfield, Laura
Hobson, Matt & Connie
Hocker, Jean
Hoffman, Nancy
Hoffman, Sue
Hoke, Liza
Holden, Marsha
Holding, Julie
Houser, Tara
Hunt, Marge
Hurlbert, Mrs. Elgin
Johnson, Fran
Johnson, Sally
Jorgensen, Jean
Keller, Lynne
Kidd, Charlotte
Kimmi, Melinda
Knori, Christie
Koedt, Inger
MacLeod, Louise
McCool, Pam
Morey, Barbara
Morgan, Wendy
Moscicki, Anna
Myrin, Bert
Nesbit, Marsha
Nicoli, Betty
Nott, Pat
Obst, Sharon
Olson, Herdis
Onyon, Eleanor
Opler, Pat
Ordway, Marge
Ortenberger, Leigh
Pace, Roxanna
Perry, Nancy

Petersen, Leslie
Phibbs, Liana
Pilafian, Peter
Porter, Cozzie
Porter, Ross
Poulson, Patty
Prazma, Billie
Ranck, Avis
Reel, Danielle
Refvem, Pat
Resor, Bill
Resor, Charles & Nancy
Riddell, Ed & Lee
Roland, Patricia
Roux, Francoise
Russell, Susan
Schneider, Peggy
Shibuya, Nancy
Shuptrine, Elwyn
Shuptrine, Sandy
Smith, Ann
Smith, Barbara
Spence, Imaging
Stark, Gail
Stearns, Dodie
Stevens, Emily
Stirn, Cara
Stirn, Cheryl
Stratton, Bonney
Sullivan, Sara
Sugden, Sue
Swift, Pam
Taleghani, Jamileh
Tallberg, Meg
Thomas, Carol
Utzinger, Jackie
Wager, Gail
Wagner, Karl & Mary
Weiss, Robin
Woodbridge, Amanda
Woodin, Jane
Yonke, Chelcie
Young, Suzanne
Zaunbrecher, Dusty
Zeigler, Dimmie

JACKSON HOLE A LA CARTE
Its Personality

Enlivening the pages of *Jackson Hole A La Carte* are recipes from Alliance members and friends of Jackson Hole from all over America, and the world, as well.

Especially chosen for their originality, they produce fare of exceptional flavor, while making use of ingredients found in most supermarkets.

The recipes have been rigorously tested. All of the dishes may be prepared in advance. As a bonus, they all may be transported easily from one location to another.

The idea of portable cuisine appealed to us because of the rise in cooperative entertaining in recent years. (How many times have you been asked to take a salad, dessert, etc. to a party?)

Our own organization utilizes this idea quite often, holding food-oriented events for which volunteers supply marvelous homemade food. These events are eagerly anticipated. After all, what is more enjoyable than gathering around food . . . and sampling someone else's creation!

The food for such occasions must arrive in good condition and "hold" well until serving time. It should be able to be served and eaten easily. All of the offerings in this cookbook meet these criteria. On page 6 there are tips on how to keep food hot or cold while in transit or while waiting to be served.

We hope that whatever your cooking needs may be, you will find as much pleasure in using *Jackson Hole A La Carte* as we have found in creating it.

From the land of wide open spaces, where the deer and the antelope still play, we wish you "Bon appetit!"

Pronghorn Antelope

TIPS FOR TRANSPORTING FOOD AND MAINTAINING ITS TEMPERATURE

HOT FOOD:

1. For the best heat retention in baked savory dishes, utilize earthenware casseroles, glass baking pans, enameled cast-iron baking vessels, or other heavy oven-to-table bakeware.

2. For dishes that are cooked on top of the stove, prepare them in flameproof casseroles from which you can serve. Alternatively, warm a casserole or other heat-proof serving dish in the oven and transfer the finished food to it.

3. In either case, immediately cover the hot dish with aluminum foil or a lid, then wrap snugly in a large, thick towel or blanket, or in several layers of newspaper. Clothespins or tape will help keep ends closed.

Food handled in the above manner will stay hot for over an hour. The one exception to this method is that the surface of food with a crisp topping should not be covered, lest it lose its crunch.

COLD FOOD:

1. If the food can be frozen, it may be transported directly out of the freezer if there is enough time for it to defrost before being served.

2. Reusable ice packs placed with food in a cooler aid greatly in keeping it cold.

3. Wrapping containers in towels or newspapers also works well for keeping food cold.

NOTE: There are a few dishes with liquid sauces represented in this cookbook. Transport them in containers with tight seals if you are concerned about spillage.

Tom's Boots

TABLE OF CONTENTS

HINTS ON INGREDIENTS FROM THE A LA CARTE KITCHEN

1. High altitude modifications are listed in parentheses in the recipes.
2. Use room temperature ingredients, unless otherwise indicated.
3. Recipes were tested using USDA "large" eggs.
4. Beat egg whites in a clean bowl with clean beaters. Bits of egg yolk or other fat in the bowl will keep the egg whites from mounding properly.
5. Use the best flavored butter available. A good brand of unsalted butter (such as Land O Lakes) is preferred for its superior flavor, especially in baking and desserts. Using unsalted butter also allows for control in the amount of salt in food. When using unsalted butter in baking, add ⅛ to ¼ teaspoon salt for each cup of flour (according to taste). (A little salt enhances the flavor of baked goods and desserts.) Margarine may be substituted for butter.
6. Butter equivalents: ½ cup=8 tablespoons or 1 stick or 4 ounces or ¼ pound.
7. Flour in these recipes refers to all-purpose white flour, preferably unbleached.
8. When baking in glass or heavy, dark pans, reduce oven temperature by 25°.
9. Start checking for doneness in baked items 5 minutes before the initial baking time is up. Ovens vary.
10. Use fresh ingredients for the best flavor, such as freshly ground pepper, freshly grated Parmesan cheese, and fresh lemon juice. Check dried herbs. If they have lost their intensity, they should be replaced. Make sure nuts are fresh. Rancid nuts will ruin your finest effort.
11. To toast nuts, scatter them on a baking sheet. Bake at 350° for 5-10 minutes, until fragrant and darker in color. Watch closely, as they burn easily.
12. Feel free to use different herbs, spices, nuts, cheeses, etc., if you prefer ones other than those listed in the recipes.
13. Whipped cream can be held for a few hours, as long as it is kept cold. Simply fold any liquid that may have accumulated in the bottom of the container back into the cream before serving. For a firmer cream, place whipped cream in a sieve lined with dampened cheesecloth. Place sieve over a bowl to catch any draining liquid.

NOTE: Many of the items prepared from recipes in this cookbook will serve more than is indicated, if they are part of a cooperative meal where many dishes are present.

Hors D'Oeuvres

Colorado Columbine (*Aquilegia caerulea*)

HORS D'OEUVRES

SAUCY SOY AND SESAME SPREAD

A sensational flavor for so little work!

3 tablespoons sesame seeds
8 ounces cream cheese
¼ cup soy sauce

1. In a heavy, dry skillet over medium heat, toast sesame seeds until golden brown (2-3 minutes). Stir often and watch closely as they burn easily. Let cool.
2. Pat seeds on all sides of the cream cheese. Place on a small, rimmed plate.
3. Pour soy sauce over cream cheese. It will form a pool around the cream cheese.
4. Serve with assorted crackers, arranged in a separate container.

8 servings

NOTE: If taking this appetizer to a party, carry soy sauce in a tightly closed container. Add before serving.

Cow Parsnip

SALMON PATE

Easily combined in a food processor, the ingredients for this delectable pate also may be blended with an electric mixer, if the Camembert is shredded first.

1 can (7¾ ounces) salmon
9 ounces Camembert cheese
⅓ cup butter, softened
2 tablespoons chopped parsley
1 medium clove garlic, minced
¼ cup chopped scallions, white part only
¼ teaspoon dried thyme, crumbled
½ teaspoon dried basil, crumbled
Salt and pepper to taste

Lemon slice and chopped parsley for garnish

1. Drain salmon. Remove skin and bones.
2. Remove rind from Camembert and cut cheese into chunks. Place all ingredients, except garnish, in a food processor fitted with the steel knife. Process until smooth, scraping down sides of work bowl as needed.
3. Place pate in a serving dish. Chill, covered, several hours to blend flavors.
4. To garnish, cover one half of the surface of a lemon slice with chopped parsley. Place on pate.
5. Serve with crackers, party rye or cut up raw vegetables.

8 servings

CURRIED CHICKEN LIVER PATE

A food processor makes this luscious pate a breeze!

1 small onion, finely chopped
3 tablespoons butter
1 pound chicken livers, cleaned and deveined
1 tablespoon cognac
3 tablespoons mayonnaise
3 ounces cream cheese, cut into 3 pieces
2 quartered hard-cooked eggs
½ teaspoon curry powder
    Salt and pepper to taste

   Parsley sprig for garnish

1. In a heavy 9″ skillet, saute onion slowly in butter until it is soft and translucent. Add chicken livers and saute until they are no longer pink. Add cognac and cook one more minute. Remove from heat. Cool 5 minutes.

2. Place mixture in the bowl of a food processor fitted with the steel blade. Add rest of ingredients, except parsley and process until smooth, scraping down side of work bowl as needed.

3. Place pate in a serving dish. Chill, covered, two hours or longer, to blend flavors.

4. Top pate with a parsley sprig. Serve near room temperature with plain crackers or sliced French bread.

8 servings

Swishing Flies

MUSHROOM AND ALMOND PATE

Nutritious, delicious, and a breeze to make in a blender or food processor.

1 pound mushrooms, sliced
1 small onion, chopped
1 clove garlic, minced
¼ teaspoon dried oregano, crumbled
¼ teaspoon dried thyme, crumbled
¼ cup butter
½ teaspoon salt
½ teaspoon pepper
   Dash Tabasco sauce
1 cup slivered almonds
2 tablespoons vegetable oil

   Chopped parsley or toasted sesame seeds

1. In a large skillet, saute mushrooms, onion, garlic, oregano and thyme in butter until liquid that mushrooms release has evaporated, about 10 minutes. Stir in salt, pepper and Tabasco sauce. Set aside.

2. In a food processor or blender, coarsely chop almonds. Remove and set aside 2 tablespoons chopped almonds. With machine running, gradually add oil to almonds remaining in machine to form a coarse paste. Add mushroom mixture to machine. Run machine until a coarse puree is formed. Stir in reserved almonds. Pack pate into a crock or small serving bowl. Sprinkle with parsley or toasted sesame seeds. Serve with plain crackers. Pate is best served the same day it is made.

8 servings

CURRIED CREAM CHEESE AND SHRIMP DOME

The method below creates a dramatic presentation. If you are in a hurry, simply combine the first six ingredients, spread in a pie plate and top with chutney and scallions.

14 ounces cream cheese, softened
 3 tablespoons sour cream
 ¾ teaspoon curry powder
 ¼ teaspoon salt
 ¼ teaspoon lemon juice
 6 ounces ready-to-eat frozen shrimp, defrosted and patted dry
1½ cups Major Grey's chutney
1½ cups chopped scallions (including tender green tops)

1. Beat together cream cheese, sour cream, curry powder, salt and lemon juice until smooth.

2. Line a small, deep bowl (2½ cup) with plastic wrap, folding excess down over sides of bowl. Pack cheese mixture into bowl, leveling top. Chill, covered, several hours or overnight.

3. Uncover cheese mixture, again folding excess wrap back. Center a 10″ rimmed plate upside down over bowl. Holding both, invert. Remove bowl and plastic wrap.

4. Cover entire surface of cheese dome with shrimp, sides touching. Spoon chutney in a ring around base of shrimp dome. Sprinkle chutney with scallions.

5. Serve with assorted sturdy crackers.

8-10 servings

Spring's Harbinger

SWISS CREAM CHEESE TORTE

This winning spread may be served simply, in a bowl, or more festively, as directed below.

4 eggs, hard-cooked
8 ounces cream cheese
2 tablespoons sour cream (approximately)
1 teaspoon dried dill weed
3 tablespoons grated Swiss cheese
Salt and pepper to taste
1 package (10 ounces) frozen peas, defrosted and patted dry

1. Mince or sieve eggs. Blend with rest of ingredients, except peas, until creamy (use a fork, electric mixer or food processor). Mixture should be fairly stiff, but spreadable. A little more sour cream may be needed.

2. Grease a 9" cake pan. Line smoothly with plastic wrap, letting edges overhang pan sides. Pack cheese mixture into pan; rap on counter to settle contents. Chill, covered, at least 4 hours (or overnight).

3. Remove plastic wrap from surface of spread and fold back over sides of pan. Center a serving plate upside down on top of pan. Holding both pan and plate, invert. Remove pan and plastic wrap.

4. Cover entire top of torte with peas (there will be extras). Surround torte with crackers or cut up raw vegetables.

10 servings

PINE STREET CLAM DIP

Simple to prepare, with a wonderful blend of flavors.

  1 **can (6½ ounces) minced clams**
  8 **ounces cream cheese**
2-3 **tablespoons minced onion**
  ½ **teaspoon lemon juice**
  ¼ **teaspoon Worchestershire sauce**
  ¼ **teaspoon Pickapeppa sauce**
    Dash seasoned salt
    Dash pepper

    Cut up raw vegetables for dipping

1. Drain clams, reserving juice. Combine drained clams with rest of ingredients, using reserved juice to thin dip to desired consistency. Place in a small serving bowl. For best flavor, refrigerate overnight before serving.

2. Serve surrounded by cut up raw vegetables of your choice.

8 servings

Ranch Gate

MAJOR GREY'S DELIGHTFUL DIP

Sweet and smoky, a cocktail hour hit!

- 1 pound cream cheese
- 2 cups shredded cheddar cheese
- 2 teaspoons curry powder
- 2 tablespoons plus 2 teaspoons dry sherry
- 1 cup peach or mango chutney
- 1 pound bacon, cooked crisp and crumbled
- 6 scallions, chopped

1. Blend cheeses with curry powder and sherry until creamy. Spread in an even layer on the bottom of a 9″ quiche dish or pie plate.

2. Spread chutney on top of cheese mixture. Top with bacon, then scallions.

3. Serve at room temperature with sturdy crackers.

12 servings

Colorado Columbine

MEXICAN FESTIVAL DIP

A layered affair to remember! This appetizer disappears in the blink of an eye.

  1 can (10½ ounces) bean dip
  3 medium-size ripe avocados, mashed
1½ tablespoons lemon juice
  ½ teaspoon salt
  ¼ teaspoon pepper
  1 cup sour cream
  ½ cup mayonnaise
  1 package (about 1¼ ounces) taco seasoning mix
  1 cup chopped scallions
  1 cup chopped ripe olives
  1 cup shredded cheddar cheese
  1 cup shredded Monterey Jack cheese
  2 cups seeded, chopped and well drained tomatoes

1. Spread bean dip on the bottom of a large, shallow, flat-bottomed serving dish.
2. Combine avocados, lemon juice, salt and pepper. Spread evenly over bean dip.
3. Combine sour cream, mayonnaise and taco seasoning mix. Spread over avocado mixture.
4. Top with successive layers of scallions, olives, cheeses and tomatoes.
5. Serve with tortilla chips for dipping.

10-12 servings

BROCCOLI WREATH WITH ROSY DIPPING SAUCE

This is lovely any time of year. The colors are especially effective during the Christmas holidays.

2 pounds broccoli
2 medium onions, finely chopped
2 cloves garlic, crushed
¼ cup butter
4 medium tomatoes (peeled, if desired), seeded and chopped
1 teaspoon sugar
1 teaspoon dried basil
1 teaspoon dried oregano
¾ cup mayonnaise
¼ cup sour cream
Salt and pepper to taste

1. Cut broccoli into flowerets. Steam until crisp-tender. Spread on paper towels to cool quickly and dry. Chill until ready to use.

2. In a 9″ skillet, saute onions and garlic in butter until soft, about 5 minutes. Stir in tomatoes, sugar, basil and oregano. Simmer 15 minutes, stirring often, or until most of moisture evaporates. Cool slightly. Whisk in rest of ingredients. Pour sauce into a serving bowl just large enough to hold it. Chill, covered, until ready to use.

3. To serve, place bowl of sauce in the center of a large plate. Surround with broccoli flowerets, forming a wreath.

8-10 servings

TAPENADE

This earthy dipping sauce will remind you of the Mediterranean.

    1 cup ripe olives (preferably Greek or Italian), pitted
    1 can (2 ounces) anchovies, drained and rinsed
    3 tablespoons capers, drained and rinsed
    1 clove garlic, crushed
    3 shallots, chopped
    3 tablespoons mayonnaise
  1-2 tablespoons lemon juice (to taste)
    ¼ cup olive oil
    2 tablespoons finely chopped fresh basil (or 2 teaspoons dried)

    Lemon slice and parsley sprig

1. In a food processor or blender, puree the olives, anchovies, capers, garlic, shallots, mayonnaise and lemon juice until smooth. With the motor running, add the oil in a thin stream until completely incorporated.

2. Remove to a bowl and stir in the basil (if using dried basil, crumble it in your hand first). Chill, covered, until ready to serve.

3. To garnish, center a thin lemon slice on the tapenade. Top with a parsley sprig. Place bowl of tapenade on a large serving plate. Surround with cut up raw vegetables of your choice for dipping.

8 servings

Bull Moose

SMOKED OYSTERS IN A SAUCE

Quick, easy, and delicious, a pearl among appetizers!

3 cans (about 3¾ ounces each) medium-size smoked oysters
6 tablespoons soy sauce
6 tablespoons lemon juice
½ teaspoon Tabasco sauce

1. Place oysters with their oil in a medium-size bowl. Combine rest of ingredients. Pour over oysters and mix well. Marinate 2-3 hours in refrigerator.

2. To serve, use toothpicks to spear oysters. Serve with French bread squares to hold the oysters. The sauce is wonderful for dipping.

8-10 servings

NOTE: The oysters in their sauce keep well in the refrigerator for several days.

Winter Hay

FRESH FRUIT WITH SOUR CREAM
GRAND MARNIER DIPPING SAUCE

Delightful for pre-brunch or pre-luncheon munching!

8 ounces sour cream
2 tablespoons orange juice
2 tablespoons Grand Marnier liqueur
1 teaspoon grated orange rind
½ cup confectioners' sugar, sifted

Prepared fresh fruit for dipping

1. Combine sour cream with orange juice, Grand Marnier and orange rind. Stir in confectioners' sugar. Place sauce in a small serving bowl. Chill 1-2 hours to blend flavors.

2. To serve, place bowl of sauce in the center of a serving platter. Surround sauce with attractively arranged fresh fruit. Use toothpicks to spear fruit for dipping.

1½ cups sauce

NOTES: This also may be presented as a salad at luncheons.
Amaretto may be substituted for the Grand Marnier.

CHEDDAR WAFERS WITH JALAPENO JELLY

Be sure to tell your guests that these fabulous thumbprint cookie look-alikes are not dessert!

½ **cup butter**
8 **ounces (2 cups packed) shredded sharp cheddar cheese**
1 **cup flour**
¼ **teaspoon cayenne pepper**
   Pinch of salt, if desired
½ **cup (about) jalapeno jelly, or red or green pepper jelly**

1. Cream together butter and cheese until well blended.
2. Mix in flour and cayenne just until incorporated. Add salt, if desired.
3. Refrigerate dough, tightly covered, until firm enough to form into balls, 1-2 hours.
4. Shape into about 48 small balls (about ¾"), and place 1" apart on ungreased baking sheets. With the end of your thumb, press a deep well in the center of each dough ball, as you proceed.
5. Preheat oven to 350° (375° at 6000'). Place a small dollop of jelly in each well in dough balls. Bake in the center of oven for about 12 minutes, until wafers are lightly browned around the edges and dry in the middle.
6. Serve warm or at room temperature. Store in a cookie tin.

48 wafers

NOTE: To recrisp, heat in a 350° oven for 2 or 3 minutes.

HOT ARTICHOKE AND CHEESE SPREAD

This is the best artichoke appetizer ever!

1 can (14 ounces) artichoke hearts, drained and chopped
1 cup mayonnaise
½ cup grated Parmesan cheese
4 ounces (1 cup packed) shredded Swiss cheese
1 teaspoon lemon juice
¼ teaspoon salt
¼ teaspoon pepper

1. Preheat oven to 300°. Mix all ingredients together. Place in a buttered, small baking dish. Cover with foil. Bake 40 minutes (or 10 minutes in a microwave oven at 70% power).
2. Serve with crackers for dipping.

8 servings

Sagebrush

HOT JARLSBERG SPREAD

You will love this warm, gooey treat!

    2 cups thinly sliced onions
    ¼ cup butter
    8 ounces (2 cups packed) grated Jarlsberg cheese
    1¾ cups mayonnaise
       Paprika

1. Preheat oven to 350°. Grease a 9″ or 10″ pie plate.
2. Saute onions in butter for 5 minutes. Combine with cheese and mayonnaise. Pour into pie plate. Sprinkle with paprika.
3. Bake in the center of oven 25-30 minutes, or until bubbly and golden.
4. Serve with sturdy crackers, party rye or breadsticks.

8 servings

Mountain Stream

CRUSTLESS CHILE CHEESE BITES

Have lots of napkins ready for this zesty appetizer!

¼ cup melted butter
½ cup flour
6 eggs
1 cup milk
1 teaspoon sugar
1 pound Monterey Jack cheese, cubed or shredded
1 can (7 ounces) chopped green chiles
1 pound cottage cheese
1 teaspoon salt
1 teaspoon baking powder
  Dash Tabasco sauce

1. Preheat oven to 350° (375° at 6000'). Place melted butter in a large mixing bowl. Using a whisk or electric mixer, beat in the flour. Mixture will be thick. Add remaining ingredients and mix well.

2. Butter a 13" x 9" x 2" baking pan. Spread mixture in pan. Bake 35-45 minutes, until golden brown and set. Cool 30 minutes before serving. Cut into 1½" squares.

16 servings

NOTE: These may be frozen after baking. Also, larger portions would be perfect for brunches or luncheons.

MATT'S MARVELOUS MEATBALLS

These saucy, piquant gems are also a main course hit. Make them larger and serve with rice.

MEATBALLS:
- 2 pounds lean ground beef
- ½ pound lean ground pork
- 2 medium onions, finely chopped
- 1 medium green pepper, finely chopped
- 1 cup chopped chives (or use ⅓ cup dried)
- 2½ cups fresh bread crumbs
- 2 eggs, beaten to blend
- ½ teaspoon cayenne pepper
- 1 teaspoon Beau Monde or salt
- 1 tablespoon Worchestershire sauce
- 1 teaspoon lemon juice

SAUCE:
- 1 bottle (18 ounces) Hunt's Barbeque Sauce (Original Recipe)
- 1 bottle (9 ounces) Major Grey's chutney
- ½ cup Worchestershire sauce
- 2 tablespoons red or white wine
- 1½ tablespoons butter

1. Line 2 or 3 large, shallow baking pans (jelly roll pans work well) with foil. Brush lightly with oil or spray with Pam.

2. Adjust oven rack to top shelf. Preheat oven to 450°.

3. Combine all meatball ingredients gently, but well. Using 1 level tablespoon of mixture, form into small balls. Place on baking pans ½" apart. Bake, one pan at a time, until lightly brown and just cooked through, 12-15 minutes. Remove meatballs to a heavy 3-quart casserole.

4. Combine all sauce ingredients in a 2½-quart sauce pan and bring just to a boil, stirring. Pour over meatballs, coating each with sauce. Cover casserole. Reheat in a 350° (375° at 6000') oven until meatballs are hot, about 15 minutes.

5. Serve from casserole with toothpicks and napkins!

12 servings

EXCEPTIONAL SALADS

Sticky Geranium (*Geranium viscosissimum*)

EXCEPTIONAL SALADS

SOMA SALAD

This Orient-inspired delight was one of the top ten recipes one year in the Los Angeles Times.

   2 tablespoons vegetable oil
  ¼ cup sesame seeds
  ¼ cup slivered almonds
   2 packages (3 ounces each) Top Ramen soup mix
   1 medium cabbage, coarsely chopped
   8 scallions, sliced

DRESSING:
   6 tablespoons rice vinegar
   1 tablespoon soy sauce
  ¼ cup sugar
   1 teaspoon salt
   1 teaspoon pepper
  ¾ cup vegetable oil

1. In a small skillet in 2 tablespoons oil, saute sesame seeds and almonds until lightly browned. Set aside to cool. Place in a large bowl.

2. Break up uncooked noodles (reserve soup packets for another use); add to bowl. Add cabbage and scallions.

3. Whisk together dressing ingredients until sugar dissolves. Toss with salad ingredients in bowl. Serve within an hour to keep noodles crisp. If making ahead, add sesame seeds, almonds and noodles within an hour of serving.

8 servings

Quaking Aspen

BROCCOLI AND CAULIFLOWER SLAW

Brightly colored vegetables in a creamy sweet and sour garlic dressing!

½ **large head of cauliflower**
½ **large bunch of broccoli**
2 **small carrots, shredded**
½ **cup raisins**

DRESSING:
3 **medium cloves garlic, minced**
2 **tablespoons mayonnaise**
⅓ **cup sugar**
1 **teaspoon salt**
⅓ **cup cider vinegar**
1 **cup whipping cream**

1. Separate cauliflower and broccoli into flowerets about 1¼" long; slice thinly. Combine with carrots and raisins in a large bowl.

2. Whisk together dressing ingredients in the order given until sugar dissolves.

3. Toss vegetable mixture with enough dressing to moisten well (not all dressing will be needed). Chill at least 2 hours before serving.

6-8 servings

NOTES: Recipe may be doubled. Dressing is also wonderful on cabbage or cole slaw.

Beaver

SUMMER SQUASH SALAD

A great use for some of summer's bounty!

VEGETABLES:
   5 medium crookneck squash (yellow summer squash), thinly sliced
   ½ cup finely chopped scallions
   ½ cup finely chopped green pepper
   ½ cup thinly sliced celery

DRESSING:
   1 clove garlic, crushed
   ⅔ cup cider vinegar
   2 tablespoons wine vinegar
   ¾ cup sugar
   1 teaspoon salt
   ½ teaspoon pepper
   ⅓ cup vegetable oil

   Leafy salad greens

   1. Place vegetables in a mixing bowl. Combine dressing ingredients.
Pour over vegetables and toss well. Chill 2-4 hours, tossing occasionally to
distribute marinade.
   2. Line a shallow serving bowl with salad greens. Remove vegetables
from marinade with a slotted spoon and place on greens. (Reserve
leftover marinade for future salads.)

8 servings

NOTE: Dressing is also marvelous on spinach salads and on cabbage for
cole slaw.

CRUNCHY BROCCOLI CHEF'S SALAD

This recipe won first place in the Pennsylvania Recipe Contest.

SALAD:
- 2 pounds broccoli
- ¼ cup thinly sliced scallions
- 1 cup sliced fresh mushrooms
- ½ cup diced cooked ham
- 3 ounces (¾ cup packed) shredded Swiss cheese
- 4 ounces crumbled feta cheese
- ½ cup toasted slivered or sliced almonds

DRESSING:
- 5 tablespoons lemon juice
- 2 cloves garlic, minced
- 1 tablespoon wine vinegar
- ¾ teaspoon salt
- ½ teaspoon pepper
- 1 tablespoon Dijon mustard
- ½ cup vegetable oil
- ¼ cup chopped parsley

1. Separate broccoli flowerets. Trim and peel stems; slice thinly. Steam broccoli parts until crisp-tender. Cool.

2. Place all salad ingredients, except almonds, in a bowl.

3. Combine lemon juice, garlic, vinegar, salt, pepper and mustard in another bowl. Gradually whisk in oil. Stir in parsley. Pour dressing over salad ingredients. For best flavor, cover and chill at least 4 hours, gently tossing salad occasionally to distribute dressing. Top with almonds before serving.

8 servings

COUNTRY GREEN BEAN SALAD

This piquant, colorful French salad has visual as well as taste appeal.

1 pound fresh green beans, trimmed and cut into 1½" pieces
2 tablespoons red wine vinegar or raspberry vinegar
1 teaspoon Dijon mustard
1 clove garlic, minced
¼ teaspoon sugar
¼ teaspoon dried tarragon
½ teaspoon salt
⅛ teaspoon pepper
6 tablespoons olive oil or walnut oil
½ cup sliced ripe olives

Salad greens
⅓ cup walnut pieces, lightly toasted
Several pimento strips

1. Cook beans in 4 quarts boiling water until just tender. Drain; then rinse under cold water to cool beans quickly. Pat dry on paper towels. Place in a bowl.
2. Whisk together vinegar, mustard, garlic, sugar, tarragon, salt and pepper. Gradually whisk in oil until well blended.
3. Add olives to beans and toss with dressing. For best flavor, chill, covered, at least 2 hours before serving.
4. To serve, place marinated vegetables in a bowl lined with salad greens. Scatter walnuts and pimento strips over the top.

6-8 servings

Fallen Aspen

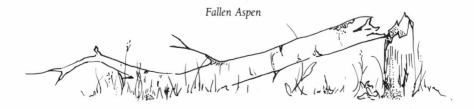

FRESH MUSHROOM SALAD

Delicate, light, refreshing!

- 1 pound mushrooms, thinly sliced
- ½ cup thinly sliced scallions
- ½ cup chopped parsley
- 1 tablespoon fresh basil (or 1 teaspoon dried)
- 3 tablespoons lemon juice
- 1 teaspoon salt
- ¼ teaspoon pepper
- ½ cup vegetable oil

Lettuce leaves and pimento strips

1. Combine mushrooms, scallions, and parsley in a large bowl.
2. Combine basil, lemon juice, salt and pepper in a small bowl. Gradually whisk in oil until well blended. Toss gently with mushroom mixture. Chill, covered, 4 hours before serving.
3. Place in a pretty bowl lined with lettuce leaves. Scatter pimento strips on top for color, if desired.

6 servings

Chanterelles

SOUTHWEST CORN SALAD

This hearty salad has an affinity for barbequed foods and meals with a Mexican accent.

1 package (20 ounces) frozen corn, defrosted
4 hard-cooked eggs, coarsely chopped
1 avocado, diced
¼ cup thinly sliced scallions

DRESSING:
6 tablespoons mayonnaise
2 tablespoons sour cream
1 tablespoon lemon juice
¾ teaspoon chili powder
¾ teaspoon ground cumin
⅛ teaspoon ground nutmeg
¼ teaspoon sugar
¾ teaspoon salt
⅛ teaspoon pepper

Lettuce leaves and chopped parsley

1. Combine uncooked corn, eggs, avocado and scallions in a large bowl.
2. Stir together dressing ingredients. Pour over corn mixture. Toss gently, but well. Chill, covered, 3 hours to blend flavors.
3. Spoon salad into a bowl lined with lettuce leaves. Sprinkle with chopped parsley. Salad is best served the same day it is made.

8 servings

ROMAINE SALAD WITH
BUTTERED BREAD CRUMBS

Grated cauliflower is the mystery ingredient in this enticing salad. People have a hard time discerning what the little white pieces are.

1 cup fine dry bread crumbs
3 tablespoons butter
1 large head romaine lettuce, torn into bite-size pieces
¾ cup mayonnaise
¼ cup sour cream
2 tablespoons grated Parmesan cheese
1 tablespoon lemon juice
1 medium clove garlic, crushed
¼ teaspoon salt, or to taste
⅛ teaspoon pepper
½ head cauliflower, grated

1. Brown bread crumbs in butter in a skillet and set aside to cool.
2. Place romaine in a salad bowl. Combine mayonnaise, sour cream, Parmesan, lemon juice, garlic, salt and pepper. Toss with romaine.
3. Top with cauliflower, then bread crumbs. Serve without tossing.

8 servings

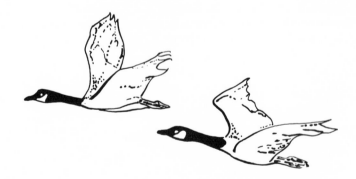

MOUSSE OF GARDEN PEAS

These simple ingredients produce an alluring flavor and velvety texture.

1 envelope unflavored gelatin
1 cup boiling water
2 cups cooked green peas (fresh or frozen)
½ teaspoon salt
⅛ teaspoon white pepper
1 cup sour cream

Small parsley sprigs

1. Place gelatin and boiling water in blender or food processor. Run machine 40 seconds. Add peas and seasonings; run machine 40 seconds longer. Add sour cream. Run machine just until sour cream is incorporated. Place mixture in a lightly oiled 3-cup metal mold. Chill until set, about 4 hours.

2. To unmold, fill sink with hottest tap water to a depth of 2". Run a knife around edge of mold; then dip bottom of mold in water for 4-5 seconds. Dry mold. Center a serving plate upside down on top of mold. Holding both, invert. Remove mold. (Repeat hot water dip if mold is stubborn.)

3. Place a ring of parsley sprigs around base of mousse before serving.

8 servings

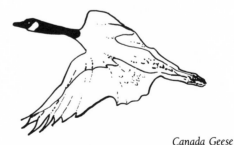

Canada Geese

ALL-AMERICAN SWEET POTATO SALAD

Originally a southern idea, this recipe came to us via Montana. It tastes very much like regular potato salad, but its looks will deceive you.

- 1 can (29 ounces) sweet potatoes or yams, drained
- 3 hard-cooked eggs
- 1 bunch scallions, finely chopped (or to taste)
- 3 medium ribs celery, thinly sliced
- 3 tablespoons sweet pickle relish
- 1 tablespoon sugar
- ½ cup Durkee's Famous Sauce
- ½ cup mayonnaise
- ½ teaspoon salt

1. Mash potatoes in a large bowl.
2. Finely chop eggs. Add to potatoes, along with rest of ingredients and stir together well. Chill, covered, at least 2 hours before serving. Salad will keep several days in the refrigerator.

8 servings

NOTE: Four fresh sweet potatoes or yams, cooked, may be substituted for the canned variety.

Roadside Grasses

WHITE BEAN SALAD WITH SAUSAGE AND ZUCCHINI

This robust salad is perfect for jaded palates. It could be a complete meal in itself.

1 pound Italian sausage, cooked and thinly sliced
1 large onion, finely chopped
1 large clove garlic, minced
5 tablespoons olive oil
1 pound zucchini, thinly sliced
3 large ribs celery, diagonally sliced
2 cans (15 ounces each) Great Northern white beans,
    drained and rinsed
1 jar (2 ounces) sliced pimentos, drained
⅓ cup wine vinegar
1 tablespoon lemon juice
1 teaspoon dried basil
1 teaspoon dried oregano
1 teaspoon dried thyme
1 teaspoon salt
  Pinch cayenne pepper
¼ teaspoon pepper

  Lettuce leaves
⅓ cup sliced ripe olives
1 small tomato, thinly sliced
  Chopped parsley

1. In a large skillet, saute onion and garlic in oil until softened. Add zucchini; cover skillet and cook over medium heat until zucchini is crisp-tender. Add celery, beans, pimentos, vinegar, lemon juice, herbs, salt and peppers, along with cooked sausage, to skillet. Heat, stirring gently, 1 minute. Remove pan from heat.

2. Serve warm or at room temperature in a bowl lined with lettuce leaves and garnished with olives, tomato and parsley.

10-12 servings

INDONESIAN RICE SALAD

*This addictive salad with its Far East flavors is adapted from one in the
Moosewood Cookbook.*

SALAD:
- 1 cup brown rice, cooked and cooled
- ½ cup raisins
- 2 scallions, chopped
- ½ cup thinly sliced water chestnuts
- 1 cup fresh mung bean sprouts
- 1 large green pepper, chopped
- 1 rib celery, diagonally sliced
- ¼ cup toasted sesame seeds
- ¼ cup toasted cashews
- ¼ cup chopped parsley

DRESSING:
- ¾ cup orange juice
- 3 tablespoons tamari or soy sauce
- 2 tablespoons rice wine or dry sherry
- Juice of 1 lemon
- 2 medium cloves garlic, minced
- 1 teaspoon freshly grated or minced ginger root
- Salt and pepper to taste
- ½ cup safflower oil
- 1 tablespoon Oriental sesame oil

- **Lettuce leaves**
- ¼ cup Chinese plum sauce

1. Combine all salad ingredients in a large bowl.
2. Whisk together dressing ingredients, adding oils last. Toss with
salad ingredients in bowl.
3. To serve, place salad in a bowl lined with lettuce leaves. Drizzle
plum sauce over the top in a random pattern. Toss plum sauce in before
serving.

8 servings

NOTE: Sliced bamboo shoots, raw snow peas, fresh pineapple chunks
and/or toasted unsweetened coconut may be added for variety.

CURRIED ARTICHOKE AND RICE SALAD

This salad is as delectable as it is easy.

1 package (6 ounces) chicken-flavored rice mix
4 scallions, thinly sliced
½ medium green pepper, diced
½ cup sliced pimento-stuffed green olives
2 jars (6 ounces each) marinated artichoke hearts
⅓ cup mayonnaise
¾ teaspoon curry powder

1. Cook rice mix according to package directions, omitting butter. Transfer to a large bowl. Add scallions, green pepper and olives.

2. Drain artichoke hearts, reserving marinade, and cut into halves. Add hearts to rice mixture.

3. Combine artichoke marinade with mayonnaise and curry powder. Stir into rice mixture. Chill, covered, 2 hours before serving.

6-8 servings

NOTE: One cup rice cooked in chicken broth may be substituted for the chicken-flavored rice mix.

Buffalo in Winter

TABBOULEH

This recipe has a Syrian heritage. It is full of nutritious vegetables and complex carbohydrates, not to mention flavor!

20 ounces (3 cups) cracked wheat (bulgur)*
2 green peppers, finely chopped
2 cucumbers, peeled and finely chopped
2 bunches scallions, finely chopped (including 1″ light green tops)
1 large bunch parsley, finely chopped
6 small tomatoes, seeded and chopped
1 cup lemon juice
1 cup vegetable oil
½ teaspoon Tabasco sauce
1½ teaspoons salt
¼ teaspoon pepper

1. Place cracked wheat in a large sieve. Rinse well under hot water until all grains are soaked. Place in a large bowl (wheat expands while marinating).

2. Add rest of ingredients to wheat in the order given, stirring well. Refrigerate, covered, 20-24 hours. This is a must in order for wheat to absorb liquid and become tender.

3. Before serving, stir salad and adjust seasonings. Additional amounts of any of the above vegetables could be used as a garnish.

16 servings

NOTE: This recipe makes a very large salad. It may be halved.

*May be found in the grain section of supermarkets or in natural food stores.

Balsamroot

MUNGER'S EXOTIC COUSCOUS SALAD

Redolent of fragrant and subtle spices, this salad will delight your taste buds.

1 box (1 pound) couscous*
2½ cups boiling water

VEGETABLES:
3 ribs celery, sliced
2 large carrots, peeled and cut into 2" x ¼" sticks
2 medium zucchini, cut into 2"x ¼" sticks
1 medium onion, halved and thinly sliced
2 medium tomatoes, seeded and diced
1 cup chopped parsley

DRESSING:
5 tablespoons white wine vinegar
1 teaspoon grated orange rind
1 teaspoon grated lemon rind
2 tablespoons orange juice
1½ tablespoons lemon juice
1 teaspoon minced garlic
¾ teaspoon ground ginger
⅛ teaspoon ground cinnamon
⅛ teaspoon ground clove
⅛ teaspoon ground nutmeg
⅛ teaspoon turmeric
1½ teaspoons salt, or more, to taste
¾ cup olive oil

1. Place couscous in a very large bowl. Add boiling water. Stir gently with a fork to separate grains. Continue stirring frequently, breaking up any lumps, until water is absorbed and couscous has cooled.
2. Add vegetables to couscous in bowl.
3. Combine all dressing ingredients, except oil, in a medium bowl. Gradually whisk in oil until well blended. Pour over vegetables and couscous. Toss gently, but thoroughly. Chill for at least 2 hours before serving.

12 servings

NOTE: This recipe makes a very large salad. It may be halved.

May be found in the grain section of supermarkets or in natural food stores.

APPLE SALAD WITH HONEY YOGURT DRESSING

A refreshing variation on the Waldorf salad theme.

3 medium Granny Smith apples, cut into small cubes
1 large carrot, peeled and shredded
2 ribs celery, thinly sliced
½ cup golden raisins
½ cup toasted pecan pieces

DRESSING:
½ cup plain yogurt
2 tablespoons honey
2 tablespoons vegetable oil
1 tablespoon white wine vinegar
1½ teaspoons Dijon mustard
⅛ teaspoon salt
⅛ teaspoon pepper

Lettuce leaves

1. Combine apples, carrot, celery, raisins and pecans in a bowl.
2. Stir dressing ingredients together; toss gently with apple mixture.
Place in a serving bowl lined with lettuce leaves. Serve within 2-3 hours.

6-8 servings

THE MAIN COURSE

Balsamroot (*Balsamorhiza sagittata*)

THE MAIN COURSE

TETON BRUNCH

This versatile recipe is wonderful when houseguests abound. It must be assembled 12 to 24 hours ahead.

12 slices firm white bread, crusts removed
3 tablespoons soft butter
2 cups thinly sliced yellow onion
½ cup butter
8 ounces mushrooms, thinly sliced
1½ pounds Italian sausage or breakfast sausage, cooked and cut into bite-size pieces
¾-1 pound medium-sharp cheddar cheese, shredded
5 eggs
2½ cups milk
1 tablespoon Dijon mustard
1 teaspoon dry mustard
1 teaspoon ground nutmeg
1 teaspoon salt
⅛ teaspoon pepper
2 tablespoons chopped parsley

1. Spread bread with 3 tablespoons butter. Set aside.
2. In a large skillet, saute onions in ½ cup butter for 5 minutes. Add mushrooms and saute until the liquid that the mushrooms expel has evaporated, 5-10 minutes.
3. In a buttered 13" x 9" x 2" baking pan, layer ½ each of the bread, onion-mushroom mixture, sausage and cheese. Repeat layers, ending with cheese.
4. Whisk together eggs, milk, mustards, nutmeg, salt and pepper. Pour over mixture in pan. Refrigerate, covered, overnight.
5. Preheat oven to 350°. Sprinkle casserole with parsley. Bake, uncovered, 45 minutes to 1 hour, until bubbly and set in the center. Let stand 10 minutes before cutting into squares to serve.

12-15 servings

NOTE: Cubed ham or crisp-cooked bacon pieces may be used in place of the sausage.

Cow and Calf

OVERNIGHT EGGS

A perfect do-ahead dish for brunches!

CHEESE SAUCE:
- 2 tablespoons butter
- 2 tablespoons flour
- 1 cup half and half
- 1 cup cheddar cheese, shredded
  Salt and pepper to taste

- 2 tablespoons chopped onion
- 2 tablespoons butter
- 8 medium mushrooms, thinly sliced
- ½ cup cooked ham, in small cubes
- 6 eggs, well beaten
- 3 tablespoons bread crumbs
- ¼ cup Parmesan cheese, or to taste
  Paprika

1. For cheese sauce, melt 2 tablespoons butter in a heavy 2-quart saucepan over medium heat. Blend in flour. Cook, stirring, for 2 minutes to eliminate raw flour taste. Remove pan from heat. Add half and half gradually, whisking briskly to form a smooth sauce. Return pan to heat. Bring sauce to a boil, whisking or stirring constantly, and cook 1 minute. On low heat, stir in cheddar cheese. Add salt and pepper to taste. Set aside, laying a piece of plastic wrap directly on surface of sauce to keep a skin from forming.

2. In a large skillet, saute onion in remaining 2 tablespoons butter 5 minutes. Add mushrooms and saute until vegetables are tender and the liquid that the mushrooms expel has evaporated. Stir in ham. Add eggs, stirring to form large, soft curds. When eggs are just set, remove skillet from heat and stir in cheese sauce. Adjust seasonings.

3. Spoon into a buttered 11" x 7" x 1½" baking dish. Sprinkle with bread crumbs, Parmesan and paprika. Refrigerate, covered, overnight.

4. The next morning, bring casserole to room temperature. Preheat oven to 350°. Bake, uncovered, 25-30 minutes, until hot and lightly browned.

6 servings

CHILE RELLENO CASSEROLE

A natural for brunch or lunch, this is an easy version of a south-of-the-border favorite.

  1 can (7 ounces) Ortega green chiles
6-8 ounces cheddar cheese, sliced
6-8 ounces Monterey Jack cheese, sliced
  4 eggs, separated
  1 can (13 ounces) evaporated milk
  3 tablespoons flour
    Salt and pepper to taste
  1 can (15 ounces) tomato sauce
    Green chile salsa, taco sauce or Tabasco sauce (optional)

1. Open chiles out flat and remove seeds. Lay ½ of the opened chiles in the bottom of a buttered shallow 3-quart baking dish. Cover with the cheddar cheese. Layer the rest of the chiles over the cheddar cheese and top with the Monterey Jack cheese.

2. Preheat oven to 350°. Beat egg yolks until blended. Stir in milk, flour, salt and pepper. Beat egg whites until stiff, but not dry. Fold into yolk mixture. Pour evenly over chile-cheese layers.

3. To tomato sauce, add a small amount of any of the optional sauces. Pour evenly over egg mixture (most of sauce will sink below egg mixture).

4. Bake, covered, 1 hour. Uncover and bake 15 minutes longer.

8 servings

Mallard Duck and Friends

MAMA'S LASAGNA

Perfect for a special occasion! This recipe may look involved, but all the components (except cooking the noodles) may be made a day or two ahead. In fact, the casserole may be assembled a day ahead and refrigerated before baking.

MARINARA SAUCE:
  1 cup chopped onion
  ½ cup finely chopped carrot
  1 clove garlic, minced
  ¼ cup butter
  1 can (28 ounces) Italian-style tomatoes, chopped
  ½ cup dry red wine
  2 tablespoons chopped parsley
  1 tablespoon dried basil
  1 bay leaf
  1 teaspoon dried oregano
  ⅛ teaspoon dried thyme
  ½ teaspoon sugar
    Salt and pepper to taste
  1 pound ground chuck
  ½ pound mushrooms, sliced
  1 pound Italian sausage, cooked and thinly sliced

1. In a heavy 3-quart saucepan, saute onion, carrot and garlic until tender. Stir in tomatoes (with juice), wine, herbs and seasonings. Simmer 1½ hours, partially covered, until sauce is thick.

2. Meanwhile, brown chuck in a large skillet (it will exude its own fat). Add mushrooms; saute until tender. Stir into completed marinara sauce, along with cooked sausage. Set aside.

WHITE SAUCE:
  6 tablespoons butter
  6 tablespoons flour
  1 cup milk
  1 cup whipping cream
  ½ teaspoon nutmeg
  1 teaspoon salt
  ½ teaspoon cayenne pepper

1. Melt butter in a heavy 2-quart saucepan over medium heat. Blend in flour and cook, stirring, for two minutes. Remove pan from heat. Gradually whisk in milk and cream to form a smooth sauce. Add nutmeg, salt and pepper. Return pan to heat. Bring sauce to a boil, whisking constantly, and cook 1 minute. Set aside, covering surface of sauce directly with plastic wrap to prevent a skin from forming.

LASAGNA FILLING:

- 2 cups cottage cheese or ricotta cheese
- ½ cup shredded cheddar cheese
- ½ cup shredded mozzarella cheese
- ¼ cup grated Parmesan cheese
- 4 egg yolks
- 2 tablespoons chopped green onion
- 1 tablespoon chopped parsley
- 1 clove garlic, minced
- ½ teaspoon salt
- ¼ teaspoon pepper
- 1 package (1 pound) lasagna noodles, cooked, drained and patted dry

1. Combine all ingredients, except noodles.

2. Spread about 2 tablespoons filling on each lasagna noodle. Roll up, jelly roll style, starting at a narrow end. You will need 18 rolls.

TO ASSEMBLE:

- **White sauce**
- **Filled noodle rolls**
- **Marinara sauce**
- ½ cup mozzarella cheese
- ½ cup Parmesan cheese
- 2 tablespoons chopped parsley

1. Preheat oven to 350° (375° at 6,000'). Butter two 9" x 9" x 2" baking pans.

2. Spread ½ cup white sauce on the bottom of each pan. Place 9 filled rolls on end in each pan. Top each pan of rolls with half the marinara sauce, half the remaining white sauce and half the mozzarella, Parmesan and parsley.

3. Bake 30-35 minutes, or until casseroles are browned and bubbly.

18 lasagna rolls

Osprey

BUTTERY SPINACH LASAGNA

The best ever! And . . . it takes less time than other lasagnas.

2 packages (10 ounces each) frozen chopped spinach,
  cooked and drained
1 tablespoon chopped parsley
2 cloves garlic, minced
2 pounds small curd cottage cheese
2 eggs
¼ cup butter, softened
⅛ teaspoon ground nutmeg
1 teaspoon salt
¼ teaspoon pepper
8 ounces lasagna noodles, cooked and drained
1 pound Monterey Jack cheese, shredded
1 cup grated Parmesan cheese
1 quart spaghetti sauce (homemade or purchased)

1. Squeeze all excess moisture from spinach with your hands.
Combine spinach with parsley, garlic, cottage cheese, eggs, butter,
nutmeg, salt and pepper.

2. Preheat oven to 350° (375° at 6000'). In a buttered 13" x 9" x 2"
baking pan, layer ⅓ noodles, ½ spinach mixture and ⅓ each cheese.
Repeat layering. On top place last ⅓ noodles and cheeses.

3. Bake, uncovered, 30-40 minutes, or until hot and bubbly. Let stand
15 minutes before cutting. Serve with heated spaghetti sauce on the side.

12 servings

Pink Wintergreen

THE INSPIRED POT OF PASTA

This is a big, hearty casserole, ideal for large, casual gatherings. Consider it when cooking for teenagers. Just looking at its cap of melting cheese will make your mouth water.

  2 pounds lean ground beef
    Vegetable oil
  1 large onion, chopped
  1 large clove garlic, crushed
  4 ounces fresh mushrooms, sliced, or 1 can (4½ ounces) sliced
    broiled mushrooms, undrained
  1 jar (14-15 ounces) spaghetti sauce
  1 can (1 pound) Italian-style stewed tomatoes
    Salt and pepper to taste
 10 ounces shell macaroni
 1½ pints sour cream
  8 ounces provolone cheese, sliced
  8 ounces mozzarella cheese, sliced

1. In a large skillet or dutch oven, brown beef in batches in a little oil, breaking beef up into small pieces. Remove from pan. Drain off all but 1 tablespoon drippings from skillet. Add onion, garlic and fresh mushrooms (if using) to skillet. Saute 5 minutes, or until onion is tender. Return meat to skillet. Stir in spaghetti sauce, stewed tomatoes and canned mushrooms (if using in place of fresh ones). Season with salt and pepper, if desired. Simmer sauce 40 minutes.

2. Preheat oven to 350°. While sauce is simmering, cook shell macaroni. Drain and rinse with cold water. Place ½ of the shells in a greased, deep 4-quart casserole or pot. Cover with ½ of the meat sauce. Spread ½ of the sour cream over the sauce. Top with the provolone cheese. Repeat layering, ending with the mozzarella cheese. Cover casserole. Bake 35-40 minutes. Remove cover. Continue baking until mozzarella browns lightly around the edges, 10-15 minutes.

12 servings

HERB-SCENTED CHICKEN TAMALE PIE

A gifted combination of flavors from the American Southwest!

FILLING:
- 1 quart chicken broth, or enough to cover chicken
- 2½ pounds chicken breast, skinned
- 3 large onions, chopped
- 2 cloves garlic, minced
- 1 bay leaf
- 1 teaspoon dried basil
- 2 whole cloves
- 3 peppercorns
- 2 canned green chiles, diced
- 1 pickled jalapeno chile, seeded and minced
- 1 cup chopped ripe olives
- 1 teaspoon chili powder
- Pinch sugar
- ½ teaspoon salt, or to taste
- 2 cups sour cream
- 8 ounces (2 cups packed) Monterey Jack cheese, shredded

TAMALE TOPPING:
- 2 cups reserved broth
- ½ teaspoon dried basil
- Pinch ground cloves
- 1 cup masa harina*
- 2 eggs, separated
- Salt and pepper
- ½ cup shredded Monterey Jack cheese
- Pitted ripe olives

1. For filling, bring broth to a boil in a deep pan. Add chicken, onions, garlic, bay leaf, basil, cloves and peppercorns. Simmer, uncovered, until chicken is tender, 20-30 minutes. Remove chicken from broth; cool. Remove meat from bones and shred into small pieces. Reserve 2 cups meat for filling.

2. Strain broth, reserving vegetables for filling (discard bay leaf and whole spices). Reserve 2 cups broth for tamale topping.

3. Combine the 2 cups reserved chicken and the reserved vegetables, along with the green chiles, jalapeno, olives, chili powder, sugar, salt and sour cream. Spread in a buttered shallow 2-quart baking dish. Top with cheese.

4. For tamale topping, bring reserved broth, basil and cloves to a boil in a heavy 2-quart saucepan over medium heat. Add masa gradually, whisking constantly, to prevent lumps. Reduce heat to low. Cook 5 minutes, whisking constantly (mixture will become thick). Remove from heat. Whisk in egg yolks. Beat egg whites until stiff, but not dry, and fold into masa mixture. Add salt and pepper to taste.

5. Preheat oven to 350° (375° at 6000′). Spread tamale topping over chicken mixture, sealing edges. Sprinkle with cheese. Press olives into topping in a decorative pattern. Bake, uncovered, 30-40 minutes, until hot and bubbly. Let rest 15 minutes before serving.

8 servings

NOTE: This pie is wonderful baked a day ahead, then reheated.

A type of corn flour found near the cornmeal in supermarkets.

Morning Coffee

SPICY HOT JALAPENO CHICKEN

Easy to make and delicious! You may adjust the "heat" to your liking.

2½ pounds chicken breast, cooked
 4 medium-size fresh jalapeno chiles, seeded and diced
   (or to taste)
 1 medium onion, chopped
 1 clove garlic, minced
 1 tablespoon vegetable oil
 ½ teaspoon ground cumin
 ½ teaspoon chili powder
 1 can (10¾ ounces) condensed cream of chicken soup
 1 package (10 ounces) frozen chopped spinach, defrosted and
   squeezed by hand of excess moisture
 ½ teaspoon salt
 1 pint sour cream
 1 package (8 ounces) corn chips
 8 ounces (2 cups packed) Monterey Jack cheese, shredded

   Paprika and chopped parsley

1. Remove chicken meat from bones; cut into bite-size pieces. Set aside.

2. In a large skillet saute chiles, onion and garlic slowly in oil until tender. Stir in cumin and chili powder; cook 1 minute longer. Stir in soup, squeezed spinach and salt. Heat to boiling. Reduce heat to low and simmer, covered, 5 minutes. Stir in chicken and sour cream. Heat through, but do not boil. Remove from heat.

3. Preheat oven to 350° (375° at 6000'). In a buttered 3-quart baking dish, layer ⅓ corn chips, ⅓ cheese and ½ chicken mixture. Repeat layering. Top with last ⅓ corn chips and cheese. Bake 30-40 minutes, or until casserole is hot and bubbly. Sprinkle with paprika and parsley before serving.

10 servings

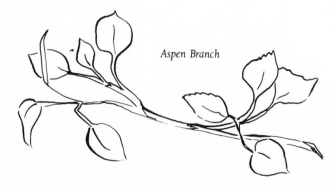

Aspen Branch

ARROZ CON POLLO
(Rice With Chicken)

This Spanish classic reached Wyoming via a stopover in Cuba. We have used boneless chicken breasts to facilitate eating at buffets.

- 1 large onion, finely chopped
- 2 large green peppers, finely chopped
- 2 large cloves garlic, finely chopped
- ½ teaspoon saffron threads, crushed in your hand
- ¼ cup olive oil
- 1 large ripe tomato, seeded and chopped (or use 3 small canned tomatoes)
- 1 teaspoon dried oregano
- 1 jar (4 ounces) sliced pimentos
- 1 cup long grain white rice
- 2 cans (10¾ ounces each) chicken broth, plus water to make 3 cups liquid
- ½ teaspoon salt
- ½ teaspoon pepper
- 8 small boneless chicken breast halves, skinned
- ⅓ cup small pimento-stuffed green olives

1. In a large skillet, saute onion, green peppers, garlic and saffron in oil until onion is tender and golden, about 10 minutes. Stir in tomato(es) and oregano; saute 5 minutes. Stir in pimentos, rice, 3 cups broth, salt and pepper.

2. Preheat oven to 350° (375° at 6000'). Ladle mixture into a lightly oiled 13" x 9" x 2" baking pan or shallow 3-quart baking dish.

3. Arrange chicken breast halves on top in a single layer. Bake, uncovered, 1 hour, or until rice is tender and broth is absorbed (scatter olives over top for last 5 minutes of baking). Let stand, covered, for 15 minutes before serving.

8 servings

NOTE: This dish is wonderful reheated.

CHICKEN FLORENTINE

Popeye would love it!

  2 packages (10 ounces each) frozen chopped spinach
  1 tablespoon butter
  1 large clove garlic, crushed
  1 teaspoon dried marjoram
  1 teaspoon dried basil
  1 tablespoon flour
  ⅓ cup half and half
    Salt and pepper to taste
    The cooked meat from 2½-3 pounds chicken breast (or from
      a whole chicken), cut into bite-size pieces

SAUCE:
  3 tablespoons butter
  3 tablespoons flour
  ¾ cup half and half
  ¾ cup rich chicken broth
  ¼ teaspoon ground nutmeg
    Salt and pepper to taste
  6 slices Canadian bacon, browned and cut into slivers
  1 cup grated Parmesan cheese
    Paprika

1. Cook spinach. Drain and cool slightly. With your hands, squeeze excess moisture from spinach. Set spinach aside.

2. In a heavy 2-quart saucepan over low heat, melt 1 tablespoon butter. Add garlic, marjoram and basil. Cook slowly 1 minute (do not let garlic brown). Stir in flour until smooth. Blend in ⅓ cup half and half and stir until thickened. Stir in spinach, salt and pepper. Simmer 5 minutes. Spread in the bottom of a shallow 3-quart casserole. Cover with chicken pieces.

3. For sauce, in a heavy 2-quart saucepan over medium heat, melt 3 tablespoons butter. Blend in 3 tablespoons flour and cook 2 minutes. Remove pan from heat and gradually whisk in ¾ cup half and half and broth to make a smooth sauce. Add nutmeg, salt and pepper. Return pan to heat. Bring sauce to a boil, whisking, and cook 1 minute longer. Stir in Canadian bacon. Pour sauce over chicken.

4. Preheat oven to 400°. Sprinkle casserole with Parmesan and paprika. Bake, uncovered, 25-35 minutes, until heated through and bubbly.

8-10 servings

SOUFFLEED FISH FOR EIGHT

A different, delectable and colorful approach to fish!

½ cup chopped onion
2 tablespoons butter
1 cup rice
2 cups chicken broth
   Salt and pepper to taste
8 thin sole fillets
4 small tomatoes, sliced
1 teaspoon chicken bouillon granules
2 tablespoons lemon juice
1 cup mayonnaise
1 teaspoon curry powder
¼ cup chopped parsley
2 egg whites
   Paprika

1. In a heavy 2-quart saucepan, saute onion in butter 3 minutes. Stir in rice and saute 3 minutes longer. Add chicken broth. Cover pan. Bring broth to a boil, reduce heat to medium and cook until rice is tender and broth has been absorbed, about 25 minutes. Season with salt and pepper to taste. Spread rice in the bottom of a buttered baking dish that is big enough to hold the fish in a single layer.

2. Arrange the fillets in a single layer on top of rice. Place tomato slices on top of fillets in a single layer.

3. Dissolve bouillon granules in lemon juice in a medium bowl. Stir in mayonnaise, curry powder and parsley.

4. Preheat oven to 350° (375° at 6000'). Beat egg whites until stiff, but not dry. Fold into mayonnaise mixture. Spread over ingredients in baking dish, sealing edges. Sprinkle with paprika. Bake, uncovered, 20-30 minutes, just until fish is cooked through (it will become opaque and flake easily).

8 servings

Lupine

BEEF AND CORN PASTEL

These contrasting flavors and textures will delight friends who love new taste sensations.

```
 5  tablespoons olive oil, divided
 3  large onions, finely chopped
 3  medium green peppers, finely chopped
 2  teaspoons minced garlic
1½  pounds lean ground beef
 1  teaspoon dried thyme
 2  cans (1 pound each) tomatoes, drained and chopped
 ½  cup chopped pimento-stuffed green olives
 ½  cup raisins
 ½  cup slivered almonds, toasted
 3  tablespoons yellow cornmeal, divided
 2  teaspoons sugar, divided
 2  teaspoons salt, divided
 ¼  teaspoon ground cinnamon
    Pinch ground cloves
 ¼  teaspoon pepper
 3  hard-cooked eggs, cut into ¼" slices
 3  cups frozen corn kernels, defrosted
 4  eggs
 1  cup milk
```

1. In a large skillet, heat 3 tablespoons oil and saute onions, green peppers and garlic until tender, but not browned, about 10 minutes. Remove to a plate.

2. In the same skillet, heat rest of oil and saute beef with thyme until cooked through, crumbling beef into small pieces. Remove from heat. Stir in ½ the cooked onion mixture, along with the tomatoes, olives, raisins, almonds, 1 tablespoon cornmeal, 1 teaspoon sugar, 1 teaspoon salt, cinnamon, cloves and pepper. Pour into a buttered shallow 3-quart baking dish. Arrange hard-cooked eggs on top.

3. Preheat oven to 350°. Puree corn in a food processor or blender until almost smooth. Add raw eggs, milk, 2 tablespoons cornmeal, 1 teaspoon sugar, 1 teaspoon salt and rest of onion mixture to corn. Pulse motor 2 or 3 times, just until ingredients are blended. Pour evenly over top of mixture in baking dish.

4. Bake, uncovered, until corn topping is puffed and lightly browned, about 1 hour. Let stand 10 minutes before serving.

8-10 servings

BABOTIE

From Africa to England to Jackson, this recipe has traveled. It was well worth the trip!

1 pound lean ground lamb or beef
1 tablespoon vegetable oil
1 large clove garlic, crushed
2 medium onions, thinly sliced
2 teaspoons curry powder
2 teaspoons ground cumin
⅓ cup slivered almonds
⅓ cup raisins
2 tablespoons white wine vinegar
2 tablespoons lemon juice
1 tablespoon brown sugar
½ teaspoon dried basil
½ teaspoon dried marjoram
   Salt and pepper to taste
2 eggs
1 cup milk

   Parsley sprigs

1. In a large skillet, brown meat in oil. Remove with a slotted spoon to a plate. In oil remaining in skillet, saute garlic, onions, curry powder and cumin until onions are tender. Return meat to skillet with onions. Remove skillet from heat and stir in almonds, raisins, vinegar, lemon juice, brown sugar, herbs and seasonings. Spoon into a buttered shallow 1½-2-quart baking dish.

2. Preheat oven to 350°. Beat eggs just until blended. Stir in milk. Pour over meat mixture. Bake, uncovered, 30 minutes, or until top is golden brown and crisp.

3. Place a border of parsley sprigs around edge of dish before serving, if desired.

6 servings

NOTE: Recipe may be doubled for larger gatherings.

WILD AND SPICY RICE AND SAUSAGE

Guests always ask for the recipe for this easy, sophisticated casserole.

1 package (6 ounces) Uncle Ben's Long Grain and
    Wild Rice mix, cooked
1 pound Jimmy Dean's hot sausage
1 cup chopped onion
1 pound mushrooms, sliced
⅛ teaspoon dried oregano
⅛ teaspoon dried marjoram
⅛ teaspoon dried thyme
¼ cup flour
¼ cup whipping cream
2½ cups chicken broth
    Dash Tabasco sauce
1 teaspoon salt, or to taste
    Pepper to taste
¼ cup sliced almonds, toasted

1. Place cooked rice in a buttered 3-quart casserole.
2. In a large skillet, saute sausage until cooked through, separating it into small bite-size pieces. With a slotted spoon, remove sausage, drain well and place in casserole with rice.
3. In about 2 tablespoons of the drippings remaining in skillet, saute onions until softened. Add mushrooms and herbs; saute 5 minutes. Add to casserole. Wipe out skillet.
4. Preheat oven to 350°. Whisk together flour, cream and broth. Pour into skillet. Bring to a slow boil, stirring, to form a smooth sauce. Pour over ingredients in casserole and stir well, adding Tabasco, salt and pepper to taste. Sprinkle with almonds. Bake, uncovered, 45 minutes, until heated through and bubbly.

8-10 servings

NOTE: One cup wild rice, cooked, may be substituted for the rice mix.

Coyote

HOLIDAY SPINACH AND SAUSAGE CASSEROLE

This robust dish attracts even those who shun spinach!

2 packages (10 ounces each) frozen chopped spinach, defrosted
1 pound lean ground beef
1 pound Italian sausage, casings removed
2 medium onions, chopped
3 cloves garlic, minced
1 pound mushrooms, sliced
1 tablespoon chopped parsley
1 tablespoon dried oregano
1 tablespoon dried basil
½ cup dry sherry
1 can (10¾ ounces) cream of mushroom soup
1 can (10¾ ounces) cream of chicken soup
1 cup sour cream
Salt and pepper to taste
8 ounces Monterey Jack cheese, sliced

1. Squeeze all excess moisture from spinach with your hands; otherwise, casserole will be runny. Set aside.

2. In a very large skillet or dutch oven, saute beef and sausage in batches until cooked through, crumbling meat into small pieces as you go. (Do not crowd pan or meat will steam, instead of brown.) Remove meat with a slotted spoon to a plate as it is cooked.

3. In 2-3 tablespoons of the drippings remaining in the pan, saute onions, garlic and mushrooms until tender and the liquid that the mushrooms expel has evaporated. Stir in parsley, oregano, basil and sherry. Cook until sherry is reduced by one half. Add squeezed spinach. Saute 3 minutes, separating pieces of spinach.

4. Preheat oven to 350° (375° at 6000'). Add cooked meats to other ingredients in pan. Off the heat, stir in soups, sour cream, salt and pepper. Spoon into a large casserole (or 2 smaller ones). Top with rows of cheese. Bake, uncovered, until heated through and bubbly, about 30-40 minutes.

12-16 servings

NOTE: Recipe may be halved. Fresh spinach, cooked and chopped, may be substituted for the frozen spinach.

PORK LOIN WITH APPLE CINNAMON SAUCE

A sweet, spicy sauce enhances a succulent rolled roast.

MARINADE:
- 1½ teaspoons ground ginger
- 3 tablespoons dry mustard
- 3 tablespoons dried thyme
- ¾ cup dry sherry
- ¾ cup soy sauce
- 3 cloves garlic, minced

- 1 pork loin roast (5½-6 pounds), boned, rolled and tied

SAUCE:
- 2 jars (10 ounces each) Cinapple jelly (or 2 jars apple jelly combined with ¾ teaspoon ground cinnamon)
- 2 tablespoons soy sauce
- ¼ cup dry sherry

1. Whisk together first 6 ingredients in a bowl large enough to hold pork roast. Add roast to bowl, turning to coat with marinade. Refrigerate, covered, 4 hours, turning roast occasionally.

2. Bring roast to room temperature. Preheat oven to 325° (350° at 6000'). Pat roast dry. Place on a rack in a shallow roasting pan. Roast, uncovered, for about 2½-3 hours, or until a meat thermometer registers 160°. Let rest 20 minutes before slicing.

3. Meanwhile, combine and heat jelly, cinnamon (if using), soy sauce and sherry in a 2-quart saucepan, whisking until smooth. Serve with roast.

8-10 servings

NOTE: To take to a party, transport roast hot out of the oven, wrapped in heavy-duty foil and then in a heavy towel. Alternatively, let roast cool. Slice before transporting. Serve cold with warm sauce. (Use a thermos bottle!)

NOT ONLY VEGETABLES

Indian Paintbrush (*Castilleja miniata*)

NOT ONLY VEGETABLES

WHITE-TOPPED ARTICHOKES, SPINACH AND MUSHROOMS

In the contributor's own words, "Here is a yummy recipe!"

1 can (14 ounces) artichoke hearts, drained and
   sliced into thirds
8 ounces mushrooms, sliced into thirds (reserve 3 whole
   caps for garnish)
5 tablespoons butter, divided
2 packages (10 ounces each) frozen chopped spinach, defrosted
1 tablespoon flour
½ cup milk
¼ teaspoon salt
⅛ teaspoon pepper
   Large pinch nutmeg

TOPPING:
½ cup sour cream
½ cup mayonnaise
1 tablespoon lemon juice
⅛ teaspoon salt

1. Place sliced artichoke hearts in the bottom of a buttered medium-size baking dish.

2. In a skillet, saute mushrooms (including those for garnish) in 3 tablespoons butter 5-10 minutes, or until tender and liquid that mushrooms expel has evaporated. Set aside the 3 whole caps.

3. Meanwhile, squeeze excess moisture from spinach, using your hands. Add spinach to mushrooms in skillet. Saute 2 minutes, separating pieces of spinach. Remove skillet from heat.

4. Melt remaining 2 tablespoons butter in a small saucepan over medium heat. Add flour and cook 2 minutes. Remove from heat and gradually whisk in milk to make a smooth sauce. Add nutmeg, salt and pepper. Return pan to heat. Bring sauce to a boil and cook 1 minute, whisking. Stir sauce into spinach mixture. Adjust seasonings. Spread mixture over artichoke hearts.

5. Preheat oven to 350° (375° at 6000'). Whisk together topping ingredients. Spread smoothly over vegetables. Top with reserved mushroom caps. Bake 25 minutes, or until casserole is hot and topping has set.

6-8 servings

SPINACH INTRIGUE

This recipe is very easy and quite dramatic!

- **2 packages (10 ounces each) frozen chopped spinach**
- **2 tablespoons minced onion**
- **8 ounces mushrooms, sliced**
- **½ cup butter**
  Salt and pepper to taste
- **1 can (6 ounces) tomato paste**
- **1 cup sour cream**
  Paprika

1. Cook spinach. Drain in a fine sieve, pressing spinach against sides of sieve to extract some of the moisture. Spread in a buttered shallow 6" x 10" baking dish or small casserole.

2. In a skillet, saute onions and mushrooms in butter until moisture that mushrooms expel has evaporated, 5-10 minutes. Season with salt and pepper. Place evenly on top of spinach.

3. Preheat oven to 350° (375° at 6000'). Spread tomato paste evenly on top of mushrooms. Spread sour cream evenly on top of tomato paste. Dust with paprika. Bake 25 minutes, or until heated through and sour cream has set.

6-8 servings

Shrubby Cinquefoil

SCALLOPED CORN AND TOMATOES

This will remind you of summer back home.

    1 cup thinly sliced onion
    ¼ cup butter
    2 teaspoons firmly packed light brown sugar
    1 teaspoon dried marjoram, crumbled
    ⅛ teaspoon ground cloves
    1 bay leaf, crumbled
    2 pounds tomatoes, seeded and coarsely chopped
    1 package (20 ounces) frozen corn, defrosted
       (or use 3 cups fresh corn)
 1¾ teaspoons salt
    ¼ teaspoon pepper

TOPPING:
    2 cups fresh bread crumbs
    2 teaspoons chopped parsley
    ¼ cup butter

1. Preheat oven to 350° (375° at 6000′). In a large skillet, saute onion in butter until tender and golden, about 5 minutes. Stir in brown sugar, marjoram, cloves and bay leaf until sugar dissolves. Stir in tomatoes and cook 5 minutes over medium-high heat. Stir in corn, then salt and pepper. Cook until corn is heated through. Spoon into a shallow 2-quart baking dish. Set aside.

2. Wipe out skillet. For topping, saute bread crumbs and parsley in butter in same skillet, stirring, until bread crumbs are golden and crisp. Sprinkle over corn mixture. Bake, uncovered, in the center of oven 45 minutes.

8 servings

NOTE: To seed tomatoes, cut in half crosswise. Gently squeeze out seeds.

CAULIFLOWER GRATIN WITH CHILES AND CHEESE

A standard vegetable becomes special in its Southwestern dress.

- 2 pounds cauliflower
- 4 tablespoons soft butter, divided
- 1 can (4 ounces) chopped green chiles, drained
- ½ cup diced onion or scallions
- 6 ounces (1½ cups packed) shredded Monterey Jack cheese or cheddar cheese
- 1 cup sour cream
- 1 teaspoon salt
- ¼ teaspoon pepper
- ½ cup dry bread crumbs

1. Break cauliflower into small flowerets. Cook until tender in boiling water. Drain. Combine with 2 tablespoons butter, chiles, onion, cheese, sour cream, salt and pepper.

2. Preheat oven to 350° (375° at 6000'). Spoon cauliflower mixture into a buttered 2-quart baking dish. Sprinkle with bread crumbs. Dot with remaining butter. Bake for 25-30 minutes, until heated through and bread crumbs are lightly browned. Do not overbake.

6-8 servings

NOTE: This recipe also may be made with cooked zucchini or eggplant.

The Grand Tetons

CAULIFLOWER PIE

A pie without pastry, redolent of garlic!

    1 large (2-2¼ pounds) cauliflower
    2 tablespoons olive oil
    4 large cloves garlic, minced, or to taste
       Salt and pepper to taste
    1 tablespoon flour
    2 eggs, lightly beaten
   ⅔ cup Italian-flavored bread crumbs
    8 ounces (2 cups packed) shredded Gruyere cheese

1. Separate cauliflower into flowerets. Steam until very tender (test with the point of a knife). Drain any liquid from cauliflower. Mash cauliflower, using a potato masher, an electric mixer or a food processor. Reserve.

2. Heat oil in a large skillet over low heat. Saute garlic slowly for 1 minute (do not let garlic brown). Add cauliflower to skillet and cook 1 more minute, stirring. Remove skillet from heat and let mixture cool 10 minutes. Stir flour, then eggs, into cauliflower.

3. Preheat oven to 350° (375° at 6000′). In an oiled 2-quart baking dish, spread half of the bread crumbs. Top with half of the cauliflower mixture, then half of the cheese. Cover with the rest of the cauliflower mixture, followed by the rest of the cheese. Sprinkle the rest of the bread crumbs on top. Bake 25-30 minutes, until hot and the bread crumbs begin to brown.

6-8 servings

NOTE: Other cheeses, such as Monterey Jack, Muenster or cheddar, may be substituted for the Gruyere cheese.

PERSIAN EGGPLANT WITH TOMATOES

This dish is superbly spiced. Some have said that this is the best eggplant dish they've ever tasted.

2 medium eggplants
Olive oil

TOMATO SAUCE:
2 large onions, finely chopped
2 cloves garlic, crushed
1 tablespoon olive oil
1 can (1 pound) tomatoes, chopped
3 tablespoons tomato paste
½ cup dry red or white wine
1 tablespoon sugar
2 bay leaves
½ teaspoon dried basil
½ teaspoon dried tarragon
½ teaspoon dried oregano
½ teaspoon fines herbes*
⅛ teaspoon ground cinnamon
½ teaspoon salt
¼ teaspoon pepper

TOPPING:
1 cup cottage cheese
½ cup sour cream
2 eggs

1. Preheat broiler. Peel and slice (½" thick) eggplants. Lightly brush each side with olive oil. Broil eggplant slices until golden brown on each side, turning once. Cut into 1" squares. Set aside.

2. In a heavy skillet, saute onions and garlic in oil until onion is tender. Stir in rest of sauce ingredients. Simmer gently 30 minutes. Sauce will thicken. Discard bay leaves.

3. Preheat oven to 350° (375° at 6000'). Place ½ of eggplant evenly in the bottom of an oiled 2½-quart casserole. Cover with ½ of tomato sauce. Repeat layering. Set aside.

4. In a blender or food processor, combine cottage cheese, sour cream and eggs. Process just until mixture is smooth. Pour evenly over tomato sauce. Bake casserole, uncovered, in the center of oven 40 minutes, or until top is golden and set, but not dry. Let stand 10 minutes before serving.

8 servings

*A prepared mixture of herbs found in the spice section of many supermarkets. Omit, if unavailable.

MONTEREY JACK'S VEGETABLE BAKE

This is a versatile recipe with a lot of eye appeal. Add or subtract vegetables at will.

      8 ounces broccoli
      8 ounces carrots, diced
      2 tablespoons butter
  1½ teaspoons minced garlic
      1 small onion, diced
      8 ounces mushrooms, sliced
      2 tablespoons soy sauce
      1 teaspoon celery salt
         Salt and pepper to taste
      7 eggs
  1½ cups milk
      1 pound Monterey Jack cheese, shredded

1. Separate broccoli flowerets. Trim stems and slice ¼" thick.
2. In a large skillet, saute broccoli stems and carrots in butter 2 minutes. Add broccoli flowerets, onion, mushrooms, soy sauce, celery salt and salt and pepper to taste. Partially cover skillet and cook gently 15 minutes, or until vegetables are barely tender, stirring occasionally.
3. Preheat oven to 350° (375° at 6000'). In a large bowl, beat eggs just to blend. Stir in milk. Stir in vegetables and cheese. Place in a greased 3-quart casserole. Place casserole in a large baking pan (2"-3" deep). Pour hot water into the baking pan to the depth of 1". Bake, uncovered, 50-60 minutes, or until center is just set. Let stand 15 minutes before serving.

8-10 servings

The Sleeping Indian

BAKED VEGETABLES WITH SOUR CREAM

Inspired vegetables! If you own a food processor, put it to use here!

  2 cups chopped green pepper
⅔ cup chopped scallions
  3 tablespoons butter
1⅓ cups grated carrots
  ½ cup minced parsley
  4 yellow summer squash, cut into thin strips
      (2″ long, ½″ wide)
  ½ teaspoon dried basil
  ½ teaspoon dried oregano
  1 teaspoon salt, or to taste
  ¼ teaspoon pepper
  1 cup sour cream
  1 cup grated Parmesan cheese, divided

1. In a large skillet, saute green pepper and scallions in butter
3 minutes. Add carrots and parsley. Saute 3 minutes longer. Add squash
and saute another 3 minutes. Add herbs, salt and pepper. Remove skillet
from heat. Stir in sour cream and ⅔ cup Parmesan.

2. Preheat oven to 350° (375° at 6000′). Pour mixture into a buttered
2-quart baking dish. Sprinkle with ⅓ cup Parmesan. Bake 35 minutes, or
until hot and squash is tender.

6-8 servings

Winter Chores

SWEET DEVIL CARROTS

This earthy root vegetable climbs to new heights in this fast and fancy recipe.

2 pounds carrots, cut into 2½" x ¼" sticks
1 teaspoon salt
3 tablespoons butter
¼ cup brown sugar
3 tablespoons prepared mustard

¼ cup chopped parsley

1. Cook carrots with salt in boiling water to cover until tender. Drain.
2. Place butter, sugar and mustard in a large saucepan. Cook over low heat, stirring, until syrupy, about 3 minutes. Add cooked carrots and toss gently to coat with sauce. Add salt, if needed.
3. Place in a heated serving dish. Sprinkle with parsley.

8 servings

HERBED ONION AND TOMATO TART

Crisp, buttery pastry holds an exceptional array of bright flavors.

TART PASTRY (PREBAKED):
- 1 cup flour
- ¼ teaspoon salt
- ⅓ cup cold butter, cut into 6 pieces
- 1 cold egg yolk
- 1-2 tablespoons ice water

FILLING:
- 1 pound onions, thinly sliced
- Large pinch sugar
- 3 tablespoons olive oil
- ¼ teaspoon dried basil, crumbled
- ⅛ teaspoon dried oregano, crumbled
- ⅛ teaspoon dried thyme, crumbled
- 1 can (1 pound) Italian-style tomatoes, well-drained, seeded and chopped
- Salt and pepper to taste
- 3 ounces (¾ cup packed) shredded Swiss cheese
- ⅓ cup pitted oil-cured olives, or ripe olives

1. For tart pastry, combine flour and salt in a mixing bowl. Cut in butter until mixture resembles coarse meal. Combine egg yolk and water. Pour over flour mixture. Stir lightly until mixture begins to hold together. (Add a little more water gradually, if dough is crumbly.) Form into a ball, then flatten into a 1″ thick disk. Wrap well and freeze 30-60 minutes, or until firm and just barely pliable.

2. Preheat oven to 425°. Roll pastry out into an 11″ circle on a lightly floured surface. Fit into a 9″ tart pan with removable sides or pie pan. Butter a 12″ sheet of aluminum foil and mold, buttered side down, into shell. Fill foil with uncooked beans. Bake on bottom shelf 10 minutes. Remove beans and foil together, carefully, then continue baking shell for 15 minutes, or until golden. Set aside on a rack. Reduce oven temperature to 375° (400° at 6000′).

3. For filling, in a heavy skillet, saute onions with sugar slowly in oil about 20 minutes, until golden and slightly caramelized. Stir in herbs and cook 2 minutes. Spread mixture evenly in tart shell. Cover with tomatoes and season well with salt and pepper. Top with cheese. Scatter olives over the top. Bake in the center of oven for 25-30 minutes, until hot and cheese is bubbly. Transfer to a rack. Serve warm or at room temperature.

8 servings

CRUNCHY-TOPPED BAKED PINEAPPLE

This is a little jewel of a recipe, homey, yet unusual. It is a nice complement to ham, turkey and pork. It even may be served as dessert.

1 **can (20 ounces) pineapple chunks**
½ **cup sugar**
2 **tablespoons flour**
6 **tablespoons butter**
5 **slices stale bread, cut into ¾" cubes**

1. Preheat oven to 350° (375° at 6000'). Drain juice from pineapple into a small saucepan before removing pineapple from can. Place drained pineapple in a buttered shallow 1-quart casserole.

2. Stir sugar and flour together until mixture looks uniform. Blend into juice in pan. Bring to a boil, stirring, and cook 1 minute to thicken sauce. Pour over pineapple.

3. Melt butter in same saucepan. Pile bread cubes on top of pineapple mixture. Drizzle melted butter evenly over bread cubes. Bake, uncovered, 45 minutes, until bread cubes are well browned.

6 servings

NOTE: Do not cover the top of this casserole if transporting it to a party, or the bread cubes will lose their crunch.

Morning Song

APPLES WITH CARAMELIZED ONIONS

A find from Luchow's in New York, this recipe offers a fresh approach to side dishes. Try it with pork or poultry.

2 **medium red onions, sliced**
2 **tablespoons butter**
6 **large tart apples, unpeeled (or peeled if desired)**
½ **cup sugar**
½ **teaspoon ground cinnamon**
   Dash paprika
1 **teaspoon salt, or to taste**

Long slivers of lemon peel

1. In a large skillet, cook onions slowly in butter for about 15 minutes, until they brown a bit and start to caramelize (stir often and do not let them burn).

2. Meanwhile, halve, core and thinly slice apples. Add to skillet, along with sugar, cinnamon, paprika and salt. Cover and cook slowly 15-20 minutes, or until apples are tender.

3. Serve in a pretty bowl with lemon peel scattered over the top.

6-8 servings

Bull Elk

MUENSTER AND
CARAWAY-LAYERED POTATOES

One of the many attractions of this recipe is that the potatoes do not have to be precooked.

½ cup butter, melted
6 medium baking potatoes, peeled or unpeeled, and
   thinly sliced
½ teaspoon salt
1 teaspoon caraway seeds (or cumin seeds)
1 pound Muenster cheese, shredded
4 eggs, beaten well to blend
¾ cup dry bread crumbs
¼ cup grated Parmesan cheese
2 tablespoons chopped parsley
1 teaspoon dried oregano
½ teaspoon pepper

1. Brush a shallow 3-quart baking dish with a little of the melted butter. Layer ⅓ of the potatoes in the dish, brush with ¼ of the remaining butter, then sprinkle with ⅓ of the salt, ⅓ of the caraway seeds and ½ of the Muenster. Repeat layering. Then add ⅓ of the potatoes, ¼ of the butter and the rest of the salt and caraway seeds.

2. Pour eggs evenly over the potato mixture.

3. Preheat oven to 350° (375° at 6000'). Combine bread crumbs, Parmesan, parsley, oregano and pepper. Sprinkle over potato mixture. Drizzle last of butter over top. Bake, uncovered, 45 minutes, or until potatoes are tender (test with a sharp knife).

8-10 servings

KAREN'S CAMP TRAIL BEANS

These are truly glorified baked beans! If you do not have a small army to feed, you may halve this recipe.

    8 ounces bacon
    3 pounds extra lean ground beef
    3 cups finely chopped onion
    2 small cloves garlic, minced
    1 cup finely chopped celery
    2 beef bouillon cubes
   ⅔ cup boiling water
 1½ cups ketchup
    3 tablespoons prepared mustard
 1½ teaspoons salt
   ½ teaspoon pepper
    2 cans (28 ounces each) molasses or brown sugar-style
      baked beans

1. In a large skillet, fry bacon until crisp. Drain on paper towels. Reserve. Drain fat from pan and reserve.

2. In the same skillet, in a little of the bacon fat (if necessary), brown beef in batches, separating it into small pieces. Set aside to drain on paper towels.

3. In the same skillet, saute onion, garlic and celery in 2-3 tablespoons bacon fat until tender, about 10 minutes. Remove from heat.

4. Preheat oven to 350° (375° at 6000'). Return meat to skillet with vegetables. Dissolve bouillon cubes in boiling water. Stir into meat mixture, along with rest of ingredients. Bake, covered, in a very large casserole for 1¼ hours. Crumble bacon over beans before serving.

16 servings

PILAFIAN'S PILAF—THE ULTIMATE VERSION

The contributor's distant relatives in Armenia were responsible for the pilaf for village feasts.

- **4 tablespoons butter**
- **1 handful fine egg noodles**
- **1 large clove garlic, minced**
- **½ cup chopped onion**
- **1 cup sliced mushrooms**
- **½ teaspoon dried dill weed**
- **1 cup white rice**
- **2 cups chicken broth**
- **½ teaspoon salt, or to taste**

¼ cup lightly toasted pine nuts (optional)

1. Melt butter in a 2-quart saucepan over medium heat. Stir in noodles and let them brown (do not let butter or noodles burn). Add garlic, onion, mushrooms and dill weed. Saute 3 minutes. Stir in rice and saute until it takes on a whitish, non-translucent appearance.

2. Meanwhile, heat the broth and salt to boiling in another pan. Pour over rice mixture and stir briefly. Cover pan tightly and simmer 25-30 minutes (steam will subside toward end of cooking time). Do not peek!

3. Remove pan from heat. Toss pilaf lightly; then cover pan, placing a dry cloth or paper towel between pan and lid to absorb moisture. Let stand 10 minutes (a very important step). Serve topped with pine nuts, if desired.

6 servings

Goldenrod

ESAU'S MESS OF POTTAGE

We hope the title piques your interest in this recipe from Lebanon. Its flavors are subtle and addictive.

    1 cup lentils, picked over and rinsed
    6 cups water
 1½ teaspoons salt
    ¾ cup rice
    3 large onions, diced
    6 tablespoons olive oil

    2 small tomatoes, seeded and diced
      Sour cream (optional, but delicious)

1. Bring lentils, water and salt to a boil in a large pot. Simmer, partially covered, over medium heat 15 minutes. Add rice and bring to a boil again. Simmer 15 minutes longer.

2. Meanwhile, saute onions slowly in oil in a large skillet for 15 minutes. Add lentil-rice mixture and simmer, uncovered, over low heat 15-25 minutes, stirring occasionally, until most of liquid is absorbed and rice is tender. Add more salt, if needed.

3. Place in a serving dish. Arrange a ring of tomatoes around edge of dish. Serve with sour cream on the side.

8-10 servings

NOTE: This dish is good hot, cold, or at room temperature and is best the next day!

UNCOMMON BREADS

Harebells (*Campanula rotundifolia*) and Grasses

UNCOMMON BREADS

CHEESE AND WINE BREAD

"Cheese and Wine" calls for a party to show off this handsome loaf.

    3 cups flour
    1 package (¼ ounce) active dry yeast
    ½ cup dry white wine
    ½ cup butter
    2 teaspoons sugar
    1 teaspoon salt
    3 eggs, lightly beaten to blend
    4 ounces Monterey Jack cheese, cut into ½" cubes

    Butter for brushing finished bread

1. Place 1½ cups flour and yeast in a large bowl. Heat wine, butter, sugar and salt until warm (125°) and butter melts. Stir into flour mixture. Blend in eggs. Mix in enough flour to form a soft dough. Stir in cheese. Turn out onto a lightly floured surface and knead about 8 minutes, adding only enough extra flour to produce a dough that is smooth, elastic and just past the point of being sticky.

2. Place dough in an oiled large crockery bowl, cover bowl with plastic wrap, and let dough rise in a warm spot until doubled in bulk, 1-2 hours. Punch dough down, shape into a round loaf and place in a greased 9" pie pan. Cover lightly with a kitchen towel and let rise until doubled in bulk, about 45 minutes.

3. Preheat oven to 375°. Bake loaf about 30-35 minutes, or until nicely browned and the loaf sounds hollow when tapped on the bottom. Remove bread from pan, place on a rack and brush with butter. Serve warm or at room temperature.

1 loaf

NOTE: This dough also may be formed into 18 rolls. Bake on greased baking sheets 12-15 minutes.

Discovery

TARRAGON POTATO BREAD

This soft bread, heady with tarragon and chives, stays moist for days.

    6 cups flour
    2 packages (¼ ounce each) active dry yeast
 1½ cups milk
    2 tablespoons sugar
    2 teaspoons salt
    2 tablespoons butter
    1 cup (part of a 10¾ ounce can) condensed cream of potato soup
 ½ cup sour cream
 ¼ cup chopped chives, fresh or dried
    2 teaspoons dried tarragon

    Butter for brushing finished bread

1. Combine 3 cups flour and yeast in a large bowl.

2. Combine and heat milk, sugar, salt and butter until warm and butter has melted. Stir into dry ingredients in bowl, along with soup, sour cream, chives and tarragon. Beat in more flour, gradually, until dough becomes too stiff to stir. Turn out onto a lightly floured surface and knead about 8 minutes, adding only as much flour as needed to produce a dough that is smooth, elastic and just past the point of being sticky.

3. Place dough in an oiled large crockery bowl. Cover bowl with plastic wrap. Let dough rise in a warm spot until doubled in bulk, about 1 hour. Punch down and divide dough in half. Shape into loaves that will fit into 2 standard loaf pans. Place loaves in well-greased pans, cover and let rise until doubled in bulk.

4. Preheat oven to 375° (400° at 6000'). Bake loaves in the center of oven for 30 minutes, or until browned and bread sounds hollow when tapped on the bottom. Brush hot loaves with butter. Remove from pans and place on a rack to cool.

2 loaves

Snowshoe Hare

EARL GREY LIME ROLLS*

The aroma of these rolls will have guests crowding into your kitchen.

　1　tablespoon Earl Grey tea
　1　cup boiling water
　1　package (¼ ounce) active dry yeast
　2　tablespoons sugar
　2　tablespoons melted butter
　1　teaspoon salt
　　　Grated rind of 2 limes (green part only)
3¼　cups flour (approximately)

Butter for brushing finished rolls

1. Place tea in boiling water. Steep for 15 minutes. Strain and cool to lukewarm.

2. Place yeast and sugar in a large bowl and stir tea into them. When yeast has dissolved, stir in butter, salt, lime rind and enough of the flour to form a dough that is hard to stir. Turn dough out onto a lightly floured surface and knead about 8 minutes, adding only enough extra flour to form a dough that is smooth, elastic and just past the point of being sticky.

3. Place dough in an oiled large crockery bowl. Cover bowl with plastic wrap. Let dough rise in a warm spot until doubled in volume. Punch down and form into 30 small (or 20 larger) rolls. Place, 2″ apart, on greased baking sheets. Cover with kitchen towels and let rise until doubled in volume.

4. Preheat oven to 375° (400° at 6000′). Bake in the center of oven 13-15 minutes. Brush hot rolls with butter. Remove rolls from baking sheets and serve immediately, or place on wire racks to cool. Serve rolls warm for best flavor.

20-30 rolls

*Recipe adapted from The Book of Bread by Judith and Evan Jones.

POMANDER BREAD

During a discussion on yeast breads, one tester suggested that a novice bread baker learn the techniques from an experienced friend. What a good idea!

- **2 packages (¼ ounce each) active dry yeast**
- **2 cups milk, divided**
- **1 cup apple juice**
- **3 tablespoons vegetable oil**
- **¼ cup honey**
- **1 egg, lightly beaten to blend**
- **2 teaspoons salt**
- **2 teaspoons grated orange rind**
- **1 teaspoon ground cinnamon**
- **4 teaspoons ground coriander seed**
- **3 cups whole wheat flour**
- **4½ cups white flour (approximately)**

1. Dissolve yeast in ½ cup warm milk in a large bowl. Stir in rest of milk, apple juice, oil, honey, egg and salt.

2. Mix orange rind and spices into whole wheat flour. Stir into liquid ingredients. Stir in white flour, gradually, until dough becomes difficult to stir. Turn onto a lightly floured surface and knead about 10 minutes, adding just enough extra flour to form a dough that is smooth, elastic and just beyond the point of being sticky.

3. Place dough in an oiled large crockery bowl. Cover bowl with plastic wrap. Let dough rise in a warm spot until doubled in volume. Punch dough down. Form into 2 loaves and place in 2 greased 9" x 5" x 3" loaf pans. Cover with a kitchen towel and let rise until doubled in volume.

4. Preheat oven to 350° (375° at 6000'). Bake loaves in the center of oven for 30-40 minutes, or until loaves are browned and sound hollow when tapped on the bottom. Turn loaves out of pans and cool on a rack.

2 loaves

Indian Paintbrush

HOLIDAY BROWN BREAD

This lightly spiced bread is good any time of the year and is delightful toasted.

1¼ cups milk
 2 tablespoons butter
1¼ cups water
 ¼ cup molasses
 ½ cup sugar
 2 teaspoons salt
 2 packages (¼ ounce each) active dry yeast
 2 teaspoons ground cinnamon
 1 teaspoon ground cloves
 1 teaspoon baking soda
6½ cups flour (approximately)

Butter for brushing finished loaves

1. Scald milk. Stir in butter and let melt. Place in a large mixing bowl. Stir in water, molasses, sugar, salt, yeast, spices and soda. Gradually stir in flour until a dough is formed that is too difficult to stir. Turn out onto a lightly floured surface and knead about 10 minutes, adding just enough flour to produce a dough that is smooth, resilient and just past the point of being sticky.

2. Place dough in an oiled large crockery bowl and cover bowl with plastic wrap. Let dough rise until doubled in volume. Punch down and form into two round loaves. Place on greased baking sheets, cover with kitchen towels and let rise until doubled in volume.

3. Preheat oven to 350° (375° at 6000′). Bake loaves 30-35 minutes, or until browned and loaves sound hollow when tapped. Remove from baking sheets, place on a rack and brush tops of loaves with butter while hot.

2 loaves

VARIATIONS: Bake dough in 2 standard loaf pans, or bake as rolls for 12-15 minutes.

PORTUGUESE SWEET BREAD

A lovely, buttery bread that tempts everyone!

   2 packages (¼ ounce each) active dry yeast
   ½ cup warm water (110°-115°)
   1 cup warm milk
   2 teaspoons salt
1½ cups sugar
   6 eggs, beaten to blend
8-9 cups flour
   ½ cup soft butter

1. In a large bowl, dissolve the yeast in the warm water. Stir in the milk, salt, sugar and eggs. Mix in 2 cups of the flour, then beat in the soft butter, 2 tablespoons at a time, until incorporated. Gradually beat in more flour until a soft dough is formed. Turn it out onto a lightly floured surface and knead about 10 minutes, adding only enough flour to produce a dough that is smooth, elastic and just past the point of being sticky.

2. Place dough in an oiled large crockery bowl. Cover bowl with plastic wrap and let dough rise until doubled in bulk, 1-2 hours. Punch dough down and divide into 3 sections. Shape into 3 round loaves. Place in 3 greased 9″ pie pans or on greased baking sheets. Cover lightly with kitchen towels and let rise until doubled in bulk.

3. Preheat oven to 350° (375° at 6000′). Bake loaves near the center of oven for 30-35 minutes, or until golden brown and bread sounds hollow when tapped on the bottom. Remove from pans and cool on a rack.

3 loaves

NOTE: Dough may be baked as rolls for 12-15 minutes.

QUICK PULL-APART STICKIES

Tender, gooey rolls with homemade taste in a fraction of the normal time!

1 loaf (1 pound) frozen bread dough
9 tablespoons butter, melted
½ cup chopped toasted pecans
½ cup light brown sugar
½ cup sugar
1 tablespoon ground cinnamon

1. Thaw bread dough, tightly wrapped, in the refrigerator overnight. When ready to use, slice loaf once lengthwise down the center of loaf. Then cut loaf crosswise into ½" slices.

2. Place melted butter in a small deep bowl. Place pecans in another small bowl. Combine sugars and cinnamon in another small bowl.

3. Butter well a 9" tube pan without a removable bottom. Dip each piece of dough into butter, then pecans and then sugar mixture. Layer in pan with pieces slightly apart. Sprinkle any remaining dipping ingredients over the top of dough pieces.

4. Cover pan with plastic wrap. Let dough rise in a warm spot until doubled in volume, about 35-45 minutes.

5. Preheat oven to 350° (375° at 6000'). Bake bread 30-45 minutes, until puffed and browned. Cool on a rack 5 minutes. Run a knife around edge of pan. Invert onto a serving plate. Remove pan. Serve stickies warm, pulling pieces apart with two forks or your fingers.

10-12 servings

Hereford Steers

JALAPENO CORN BREAD

Spicy and moist, full of melting cheese, this is cornbread the way Westerners like it.

⅔ cup safflower oil
2 eggs, lightly beaten
8 ounces sour cream
1 can (16 ounces) creamed corn
¼ cup minced onion
¼ cup minced red or green bell pepper
1-2 jalapeno peppers, minced
1½ cups yellow cornmeal
2 teaspoons (1 teaspoon at 6000′) baking powder
1 teaspoon salt
6 ounces shredded (1½ cups packed) sharp cheddar cheese

1. Preheat oven to 350° (375° at 6000′). Oil a 9″ ovenproof skillet or 9″ x 9″ x 2″ baking pan. Mix together oil, eggs, sour cream, corn, onion, bell pepper and jalapeno(s) in a bowl.

2. Combine cornmeal, baking powder and salt in a large bowl. Pour in the liquid ingredients and mix briefly, just to blend, leaving a few lumps. Pour ½ of the batter into the prepared pan. Top with the cheese. Top evenly with remaining batter.

3. Bake about 40-45 minutes, just until top springs back when lightly touched. Cool briefly on a rack before serving with lots of butter.

8-10 servings

Cattle and Aspens

CHEESE-STUDDED CARAWAY RYE MUFFINS

A quick fix with a surprise inside, these little breads make an impressive showing at any gathering.

 1 cup rye flour
 2/3 cup white flour
 1½ teaspoons (¾ teaspoon at 6000') baking powder
 ½ teaspoon (¼ teaspoon at 6000') baking soda
 ½ teaspoon salt
 ½ teaspoon caraway seeds
 ½ teaspoon poppy seeds
 6 tablespoons chopped walnuts
 2 eggs, lightly beaten to blend
 2 tablespoons honey
 ¼ cup vegetable oil
 1 cup buttermilk
 12 cubes (¾″) of cheese of your choice (cream cheese, Monterey Jack, Swiss, Muenster, etc.)

1. Preheat oven to 400° (425° at 6000'). In a mixing bowl, stir together the flours, baking powder, baking soda, salt, caraway and poppy seeds and walnuts.

2. In another bowl, stir together the eggs and honey until the honey is incorporated. Blend in oil and buttermilk. Pour all at once into dry ingredients. With a rubber spatula or large spoon, gently fold ingredients together just until flour is moistened, leaving a few lumps. Overmixing will cause tough muffins. Divide batter among 12 standard (2½″) well-greased muffin cups. Gently press a cheese cube into the center of each. Top of cheese may show. Bake in the center of oven 18-20 minutes, until puffed and browned. Remove muffins from cups and place on wire racks to cool. Serve warm or at room temperature.

12 muffins

NOTE: Try these as "muffin-wiches" for picnics.

CHAMELEON PUMPKIN BREAD

. . . Chameleon because of the different personalities this wonderful tea bread takes on by varying the vegetable or fruit.

3 cups flour
1 teaspoon ground cinnamon
1 teaspoon ground nutmeg
1 teaspoon ground allspice
1 teaspoon ground cloves
1 teaspoon (½ teaspoon at 6000') baking powder
1 teaspoon (½ teaspoon at 6000') baking soda
¾ teaspoon salt
2 cups sugar
1 cup vegetable oil
3 eggs
1 teaspoon orange or vanilla extract
1 can (1 pound) pumpkin
1 cup chopped toasted pecans or walnuts

1. Preheat oven to 350° (375° at 6000'). Stir together flour, spices, baking powder, baking soda and salt in a bowl. Set aside.

2. Beat together sugar, oil, eggs and extract until creamy. Mix in pumpkin. Gently blend in flour mixture in 3 additions, just until incorporated. Gently fold in nuts. Pour into 2 buttered standard loaf pans.

3. Bake in the center of oven 50-60 minutes, or until a toothpick inserted in the center comes out just clean. Cool on a rack 20 minutes, then turn out of pans and cool before slicing.

2 loaves

VARIATIONS: In place of the pumpkin, try 1 pound of shredded zucchini, apples or pears. For a blueberry edition, add 1 pound of blueberries (defrosted frozen berries are fine) to the batter after the second addition of flour.

POPPY SEED SUGAR LOAVES

This almond flavored tea bread has a fine texture. It slices beautifully.

  3 cups flour
  ½ teaspoon salt
1½ teaspoons (¾ teaspoon at 6000') baking powder
  2 tablespoons poppy seeds
  2 cups sugar
1½ cups vegetable oil
  3 eggs
1½ teaspoons vanilla extract
1½ teaspoons almond extract
1½ cups milk

GLAZE:
  ¼ cup orange juice
  ½ cup sugar
  ½ teaspoon almond extract

1. Preheat oven to 350° (375° at 6000'). Stir together flour, salt, baking powder and poppy seeds in a bowl. Set aside.

2. Beat together sugar, oil, eggs and extracts until creamy. Gently blend in dry ingredients in 3 additions, alternating with milk, beginning and ending with dry ingredients. Do not overmix. Pour batter into 2 buttered standard loaf pans.

3. Bake in the center of oven 50-60 minutes, or until a toothpick inserted in the center of a loaf comes out clean. Place on a rack to cool.

4. While bread is baking, combine glaze ingredients in a small bowl, stirring to dissolve sugar as much as possible. Brush glaze over hot loaves. Cool before removing from pans.

2 loaves

Pika and Phlox

Sour Cream Coffee Cake

Tender, moist, with a hint of cinnamon, this is what coffee cake is all about.

TOPPING:
- 1 cup chopped toasted pecans or walnuts
- 2 teaspoons ground cinnamon
- ½ cup sugar

BATTER:
- 3 cups flour
- 3 teaspoons (1½ teaspoons at 6000′) baking powder
- 1 teaspoon (½ teaspoon at 6000′) baking soda
- ½ teaspoon salt
- 1 cup butter
- 1 cup sugar
- 3 eggs
- 1 teaspoon vanilla
- 1½ cups sour cream
- ½ cup water

1. Mix together topping ingredients. Set aside.
2. Stir together flour, baking powder, baking soda and salt. Set aside.
3. Cream butter and sugar until light and fluffy. Beat in eggs, one at a time, until well blended. Add vanilla. Gently blend in dry ingredients in 3 additions, alternating with sour cream and water, beginning and ending with dry ingredients. Do not overmix.
4. Preheat oven to 350° (375° at 6000′). Pour ½ of the batter into a well buttered 12 cup Bundt pan. Sprinkle with ½ of the topping. Cover with the rest of the batter, then the rest of the topping.
5. Bake in the center of oven 50-55 minutes, or until a toothpick inserted in the center comes out just clean. Cool on a rack to lukewarm. Unmold onto a serving plate.

16 servings

SOUR CHERRY KUCHEN

Bursting with flavor, this is rather like a fruit quiche—and real men will love it!

CRUST:
- ½ cup cold butter, cut into 8 slices
- 2 cups flour
- ¼ cup sugar
- ¼ teaspoon baking powder
- ¼ teaspoon salt

FILLING:
- 1 can (1 pound) tart red cherries packed in water, well drained
- ¾ cup sugar
- 1½ teaspoons ground cinnamon
- 1 egg, lightly beaten
- 1 cup whipping cream

1. Preheat oven to 400° (425° at 6000′). For crust, cut butter into dry ingredients until mixture resembles fine meal. Press onto the bottom and up the sides of an 11″ tart pan with removable sides.

2. Gently scatter cherries over the top of the crust. Combine ¾ cup sugar with the cinnamon and pour evenly over the cherries. Bake in the center of oven 15 minutes. Remove from oven.

3. Blend egg and cream together. Pour carefully over cherry mixture. Bake 25 minutes longer, until golden brown. Cool to lukewarm on a rack before serving.

8 servings

NOTES: A 13″ x 9″ x 2″ baking pan may be used in place of the tart pan. The crust may be made in a food processor using frozen butter.

Raven

BLUEBERRY BUCKLE

A tender, rich cake, ladened with fruit, under a crunchy, bumpy cap!

TOPPING:
- ½ cup sugar
- ⅓ cup flour
- ½ teaspoon cinnamon
- ½ cup chopped toasted pecans, walnuts or almonds
- 3 tablespoons soft butter

BATTER:
- 1½ cups flour
- 2 teaspoons (1 teaspoon at 6000') baking powder
- ¼ teaspoon salt
- ½ cup butter
- ¾ cup sugar
- 1 egg
- ½ cup orange juice or milk
- 12 ounces (2 cups) fresh or defrosted frozen blueberries, or
  1 can (14 ounces) blueberries

1. Blend topping ingredients together with a pastry blender, fork or food processor until crumbly. Set aside.

2. Stir together flour, baking powder and salt. Set aside.

3. Cream butter and sugar until light and fluffy. Beat in egg. Gently blend in dry ingredients alternately with orange juice, beginning and ending with dry ingredients. Do not overmix. Drain defrosted or canned blueberries. Gently fold berries into batter.

4. Preheat oven to 350° (375° at 6000'). Spread batter in a buttered 9" x 9" x 2" baking pan. Sprinkle evenly with topping. Bake in the center of oven for about 45 minutes, until a toothpick inserted in the center comes out just clean. Cool on a rack.

9 servings

SOUTH PARK RHUBARB COFFEE CAKE

This recipe makes good use of one of springtime's culinary delights.

TOPPING:
- ¼ cup brown sugar
- 1 teaspoon ground cinnamon
- ½ cup chopped toasted pecans or walnuts

BATTER:
- 1 cup white flour
- 1 cup whole wheat flour
- 1 teaspoon (½ teaspoon at 6000′) baking soda
- 2 teaspoons ground cinnamon
- ½ teaspoon ground allspice
- ½ teaspoon ground cloves
- ½ teaspoon salt
- 1⅓ cups sugar
- ½ cup vegetable oil
- 2 eggs
- ⅓ cup milk
- 2¾ cups diced raw rhubarb (fresh or frozen, defrosted)

1. Preheat oven to 350° (375° at 6000′). Combine topping ingredients. Set aside.

2. Stir together flours, baking soda, spices and salt. Set aside.

3. Beat together the sugar, oil and eggs until creamy. Stir in milk. Gently blend in dry ingredients just until flour disappears. Fold in rhubarb. Pour into a buttered 13″ x 9″ x 2″ baking pan. Sprinkle with topping.

4. Bake in the center of oven about 35 minutes, or until a toothpick inserted in the center comes out just clean. Cool on a rack.

12 servings

Uinta Ground Squirrel

CRANBERRY UPSIDE DOWN COFFEE CAKE

Try this for your next brunch. It is quick, easy and memorable.

TOPPING:
- 2 cups cranberries
- ½ cup chopped toasted pecans or walnuts
- ½ cup sugar

CAKE:
- 1 cup flour
- 1 cup sugar
- ½ cup butter, melted
- ¼ cup vegetable oil
- ⅛ teaspoon salt
- 2 eggs, beaten to blend

Sweetened or unsweetened whipped cream

1. Preheat oven to 325° (350° at 6000′). Place cranberries in the bottom of a well buttered 9″ pie plate. Sprinkle with nuts, then sugar. Set aside.

2. Gently stir together cake ingredients until blended. Pour evenly over cranberry mixture and spread gently. Bake in the center of oven about 45 minutes, or until golden brown and a toothpick inserted in the center of cake comes out just clean. Let cool on a rack 20 minutes. Run a knife around edge of cake. Invert onto a serving plate. Serve warm with whipped cream, if desired.

8 servings

DESSERTS TO DELIGHT

Cow Parsnip (*Heracleum sphondylium*)

DESSERTS TO DELIGHT

CHOCOLATE HEAVEN

The paramount chocolate dessert! If you are not familiar with some European tortes, do not be surprised when this one subsides in the center.

- 11 ounces semi-sweet chocolate
- 5 tablespoons strong coffee (liquid)
- 1 cup butter
- 2 cups sugar
- 1 teaspoon vanilla extract
- 6 eggs, separated
- 1 cup flour

GLAZE (OPTIONAL):
- 4 ounces semi-sweet chocolate
- ¼ cup butter

Unsweetened whipped cream

1. Preheat oven to 350° (375° at 6000'). Melt chocolate and coffee together in a double boiler or heavy saucepan over very low heat. Stir gently to blend. Set aside.

2. Cream butter and sugar until light and fluffy. Add vanilla. Add egg yolks, one at a time, beating until combined after each addition. Gently blend in flour, just until incorporated. Set aside.

3. Beat egg whites until stiff, but not dry. Fold chocolate mixture and egg whites together. Then fold chocolate mixture into butter/flour mixture. Do not overmix. Gently pour batter into a buttered and floured 9" springform pan.

4. Bake in the center of oven 60-65 minutes. When done, the top will be crusty and the center will be very moist. Do not overbake. Place torte on a rack and immediately run a sharp knife around the edge of torte to loosen it. Top will crack and torte will sink while cooling.

5. Remove pan sides from cooled torte. Dust top of torte with confectioners' sugar before serving. Alternatively, use glaze.

6. For glaze, melt chocolate and butter together. Let cool until just pourable. Invert torte onto a serving plate. Remove bottom of pan. Pour glaze onto the center of the torte. Spread toward the edges, letting a little of the glaze run part way down the sides. Serve with whipped cream.

12 servings

JOSEHIND

This lemon-scented coconut delight from the Middle East is almost more a confection than a cake. Serve it in small pieces with lots of steaming coffee.

SYRUP:
2½ cups sugar
¾ cup water
1 tablespoon lemon juice

CAKE:
2¼ cups sifted flour (sift before measuring)
2 teaspoons (1 teaspoon at 6000') baking powder
¼ teaspoon salt
1 cup butter
¾ cup sugar
4 eggs
1½ cups shredded coconut
2 teaspoons grated lemon rind
1¼ cups milk

FROSTING:
8 ounces cream cheese
1 tablespoon confectioners' sugar
1 teaspoon vanilla extract
3-4 tablespoons milk (optional, for thinning frosting)

1. For syrup, bring sugar, water and lemon juice to a boil in a heavy 2-quart sauce pan over medium-high heat, stirring to dissolve sugar. Let syrup boil 1 minute. It will become clear. Set aside to cool.

2. Preheat oven to 350° (375° at 6000'). For cake, combine flour, baking powder and salt. Set aside. Cream butter and sugar until light and fluffy. Beat in eggs one at a time. Mix in coconut and lemon rind. Gently blend in flour mixture alternately with milk, beginning and ending with flour mixture. Do not overmix. Pour into a buttered 15½" x 10½" x 1½" baking pan. Bake in the center of oven 25-27 minutes, or until cake is golden brown and shrinks away from the sides of the pan.

3. Place cake on a rack. Pour cooled syrup slowly and evenly over top of hot cake. Let cool.

4. For frosting, cream together cream cheese, confectioners' sugar and vanilla. Place in a pastry bag with a ¼" star tip. Pipe crisscrossing diagonal lines, about 2½" apart, over surface of cake. Alternatively, thin frosting with a little milk until it falls in a heavy ribbon from a spoon. Drizzle in a heavy stream in a random pattern over cake, leaving some open spaces.

20 servings

PINEAPPLE CAKE WITH CREAM CHEESE FROSTING

As easy as it is good, this cake will delight even those who are not fond of pineapple.

CAKE:
- 2 cups flour
- 2 cups sugar
- 2 teaspoons baking soda
- ½ teaspoon salt
- 2 eggs, beaten to blend
- 1 teaspoon vanilla extract
- 1 cup chopped toasted pecans or walnuts
- 1 can (20 ounces) crushed pineapple, with its juice

FROSTING:
- 8 ounces cream cheese
- ½ cup butter
- 1½ cups confectioners' sugar
- 1 teaspoon vanilla extract

    Whole or chopped nuts

1. Preheat oven to 350° (375° at 6000′). In a large bowl, gently mix all cake ingredients together by hand. Pour into an ungreased 13″ x 9″ x 2″ baking pan. Bake 30-40 minutes, until the top springs back when lightly touched and a toothpick inserted in the center comes out just clean. Cool on a rack.

2. For frosting, beat together cream cheese and butter until smooth. Gradually blend in confectioners' sugar and vanilla. Beat until fluffy. Spread on cool cake. Arrange nuts on top to suit your fancy.

15 servings

Barn in Winter

FOOD FOR THE GODS

This must have come from the Garden of Eden.

2 cups sugar
6 eggs, separated
1 pound walnuts, broken into small pieces
8 ounces pitted dates, snipped into small pieces
7 tablespoons cracker crumbs (Saltines or Ritz)
2 teaspoons (1 teaspoon at 6000′) baking powder

Unsweetened whipped cream

1. Preheat oven to 325° (350° at 6000′). In a mixing bowl, gradually add sugar to egg yolks, beating until thick and light in color. Fold in walnuts, dates and cracker crumbs mixed with baking powder.

2. Beat egg whites until stiff, but not dry. Fold into walnut mixture. Spread evenly in 2 buttered and floured 8″ x 8″ x 2″ baking pans. Bake in the center of oven about 50 minutes, or until tooth pick inserted in the center of cake comes out clean. Cool on a rack.

3. Cut into small squares. Cake may be a little sticky. This is natural. Serve with unsweetened whipped cream.

32 squares

NOTE: Recipe may be halved.

Clark's Nutcracker

THE GIRDLE BUSTER

A devastating coffee cheesecake, enhanced by chocolate!

CRUST:
1¼ cups graham cracker crumbs
¼ cup sugar
¼ cup melted butter

FILLING:
1½ pounds cream cheese
1 cup sugar
3 eggs
1 teaspoon vanilla
1½ teaspoons instant coffee dissolved in ½ teaspoon warm water

TOPPING:
6 ounces semi-sweet or sweet chocolate
½ cup sour cream

1. Preheat oven to 350°. Combine crust ingredients and press onto the bottom and 1″ up the sides of a 9″ springform pan. Bake 10 minutes, or until lightly browned. Set on a rack.

2. For filling, beat cream cheese and sugar until smooth and creamy. Gently mix in eggs, one at a time, just until blended. Stir in vanilla and coffee. Pour into crust. Bake 40-45 minutes, or until center of cheesecake jiggles only slightly when pan is shaken. Place on a rack to cool.

3. For topping, melt chocolate with sour cream in a double boiler or heavy saucepan over very low heat, stirring gently to blend. Pour onto center of cooled cheesecake and spread carefully to within ½″ of the edge. Refrigerate overnight before serving. Remove pan sides before serving.

12 servings

PUMPKIN CHEESECAKE

A nice change from pumpkin pie for the holidays, but do not wait until Thanksgiving to try it!

CRUST:
- 1 cup graham cracker crumbs
- ¼ cup crushed ginger snaps
- ¼ cup sugar
- ¼ cup melted butter

FILLING:
- 1½ pounds cream cheese
- 1 cup light brown sugar
- ½ cup sugar
- 5 eggs
- 1 can (1 pound) pumpkin
- 1 teaspoon ground cinnamon
- ¼ teaspoon ground nutmeg
- ¼ teaspoon ground cloves
- ¼ cup whipping cream

CARAMELIZED WALNUTS:
- ¼ cup butter
- ½ cup light brown sugar
- 1 teaspoon lemon juice
- 1 cup perfect walnut halves

1. Preheat oven to 350°. Combine crust ingredients and press onto the bottom and 1" up the sides of a 9" springform pan. Bake 10 minutes, or until lightly browned. Set on a rack. Lower oven temperature to 325°.

2. For filling, beat together cream cheese and sugar until smooth and creamy. Gently mix in eggs, one at a time, until blended. Mix in pumpkin, spices and cream. Pour into crust. Bake in the center of oven 1½ hours. Turn off oven and allow cheesecake to remain in oven with door closed 30 minutes longer. Place on a rack to cool.

3. For caramelized walnuts, bring butter, sugar and lemon juice slowly to a boil in a heavy saucepan, stirring to dissolve sugar. Stir in walnuts and let mixture boil slowly 5 minutes. Remove from heat. Decorate top of cooled cheesecake with caramelized walnuts. Refrigerate overnight before serving.

12-16 servings

R Lazy S Brown Sugar Cheesecake

Pamper your friends with this unusually flavored cheesecake.

CRUST:
- 1¼ cups graham cracker crumbs
- ¼ cup sugar
- ½ teaspoon cinnamon
- ¼ cup melted butter

FILLING:
- 2 pounds cream cheese
- ¾ cup plus 2 tablespoons light brown sugar, divided
- ¾ cup sugar
- 1 teaspoon vanilla
- 1 tablespoon flour
- 3 eggs
- 1 cup toasted pecan pieces

1. Preheat oven to 350°. Combine crust ingredients and press onto the bottom and 1″ up the sides of a 9″ springform pan. Bake 10 minutes, or until lightly browned. Place on a rack.

2. For filling, beat together cream cheese, ¾ cup brown sugar and sugar until smooth and creamy. Blend in vanilla and flour. Gently mix in eggs, one at a time, just until blended. Mix in pecans. Pour batter into crust. Sprinkle with 2 tablespoons brown sugar.

3. Bake in the center of oven 50-60 minutes, or until center of cheesecake jiggles just slightly when pan is shaken. Cool on a rack. Refrigerate overnight before serving.

12-16 servings

Golden-mantled Ground Squirrel

FANCY FUDGE PIE

Raspberries and chocolate, a European tradition and an American favorite!

   2 ounces unsweetened chocolate
   ½ cup butter
   1 cup sugar
   1 teaspoon vanilla extract
   2 eggs, well beaten to blend
   ½ cup cake flour
3-4 tablespoons seedless raspberry preserves
   1 cup whipping cream

   Grated semi-sweet chocolate

1. Preheat oven to 300° (325° at 6000′). In a heavy 2-quart saucepan, melt chocolate with butter over low heat. Remove from heat and stir in sugar and vanilla. Gradually stir in eggs. Sift flour over batter and gently blend in. Do not overmix. Pour into a buttered 9″ pie pan. Bake in the center of oven 25-30 minutes, or until a toothpick inserted in the center of pie comes out just clean. Cool on a rack.

2. Beat preserves to loosen consistency. Spread over pie.

3. Whip cream until stiff. Spread over pie within a couple hours of serving, or serve on the side. Dust with grated chocolate, if desired.

8 servings

NOTE: Pie may be served without preserves or whipped cream.

End of the Trail

GLAZED STRAWBERRY AND CHOCOLATE TART

Ooh, ahh, mmm . . . Take our words for it!

ALMOND SHORT CRUST:
  6 tablespoons butter
  2 tablespoons sugar
  ¼ teaspoon salt
  1 egg yolk
  1 teaspoon grated lemon rind
  1 teaspoon vanilla extract
  1 tablespoon almond extract
  ¾ cup plus 2 tablespoons sifted flour
  ⅔ cup finely chopped toasted blanched almonds

FILLING:
  6 ounces semi-sweet chocolate
  3 tablespoons butter
  4 pints large fresh strawberries
  ½ cup strained apricot preserves

  Lightly sweetened whipped cream

1. For crust, cream butter, sugar, salt, egg yolk, lemon rind and extracts until smooth. Mix in flour and almonds just until a crumbly dough forms. Pat dough into a 1″ thick disk. Cover tightly and freeze 30-60 minutes, until dough is firm, but still pliable. Butter, or spray with Pam, an 11″ tart pan with removable sides. With floured fingers, press dough onto pan bottom and up the sides. Chill unbaked crust, covered, 2 hours; or freeze, covered, 1 hour.

2. Preheat oven to 375° (400° at 6000′). Bake crust in the center of oven 20-25 minutes, until golden brown, piercing any air bubbles with a sharp knife. Cool on a rack before filling.

3. For filling, melt chocolate and butter together in a heavy saucepan over low heat. Pour into crust and spread evenly over bottom. Choosing similarly sized berries, gently press berries, stem end down, into chocolate, one at a time, arranging them, sides touching, in concentric circles, working from the edge of the crust toward the center.

4. Melt preserves over low heat, stirring. With a pastry brush or spoon, glaze each berry with preserves, using as much of the preserves as needed. Chill tart at least 2 hours before serving. Tart is best served the same day it is made. Serve with lightly sweetened whipped cream.

10 servings

COFFEE WALNUT TART

A perfect union of flavors and textures. You may want to keep it all to yourself!

TART PASTRY:
- 1 cup flour
- 1 tablespoon sugar
- ¼ teaspoon salt
- 6 tablespoons cold butter, cut into small pieces
- 1 cold egg yolk, slightly beaten
- 1 tablespoon ice water

FILLING:
- 1⅓ cups walnuts
- ¾ cup sugar
- ½ cup soft butter, cut into 4 pieces
- 2 eggs
- 1 teaspoon instant coffee dissolved in 3 tablespoons hot water
- ⅛ teaspoon salt

ICING:
- 1 cup confectioners' sugar
- 1 teaspoon vanilla extract
- ¾ teaspoon instant coffee dissolved in 2 tablespoons hot water

12 walnut halves

1. For tart pastry, combine flour, sugar and salt in a mixing bowl. Cut in butter until mixture resembles coarse meal. Combine egg yolk and water. Pour over flour mixture, tossing ingredients lightly with a fork, just until dough begins to cling together. If dough is crumbly, add a little more ice water, gradually. Gather dough into a ball. Flatten it into a 1" thick disk. Freeze, tightly wrapped, for 30-60 minutes, until dough is firm and barely pliable.

2. Preheat oven to 375° (400° at 6000'). Roll dough out into an 11"-12" circle. Fit into a 9" springform pan, pie pan or cake pan (preferably one with removable sides). Build up edges 1¾" high. Set aside in refrigerator while making filling.

3. For filling, combine walnuts and sugar in a food processor or blender. Process until mixture is fine textured. Add butter, eggs, coffee and salt. Process until mixture is smooth. Pour into tart shell. Bake in the center of oven 25-35 minutes, or until a knife inserted in the center of tart comes out clean. Cool completely on a rack.

4. For icing, combine confectioners' sugar with vanilla and enough coffee to make an icing that is just fluid. Spread over tart to within ½" of the edge. Place walnut halves in a circle on tart just inside the edge of icing.

8 servings

BROWN BEAUTIES

Chocolate morsels that will outshine the best of them on the dessert table! They are a snap to prepare.

  4 ounces unsweetened chocolate
  1 cup butter
1½ cups chopped toasted pecans
1¾ cups sugar
  1 cup flour
  4 eggs, beaten to blend
  1 teaspoon vanilla

1. Preheat oven to 350° (375° at 6000′). In a large, heavy saucepan over low heat, melt chocolate with butter. Remove from heat. Stir in pecans.

2. While chocolate and butter are melting, stir sugar and flour together in a mixing bowl until mixture is uniform. Pour in beaten eggs and vanilla and gently fold ingredients together just until blended. Overmixing will cause tough cupcakes. Gently blend flour mixture into chocolate mixture.

3. Spoon batter into 18 standard muffin cups that have been sprayed with Pam or lined with paper baking cups. Bake in the center of oven 25-30 minutes, or until a toothpick inserted in the center of a cupcake comes out with just a crumb or two clinging to it. Do not overbake. Cool on a wire rack.

18 cupcakes

NOTE: To further delight the chocoholic, try adding 1 cup white chocolate, milk chocolate or semi-sweet chocolate chips to the batter.

Trumpeter Swan and Cygnets

RASPBERRY CREAM BARS OR TART

Sweet smelling of preserves and almond paste, this is a dessert over which to linger.

CRUST:
- 1 **cup butter**
- ½ **cup confectioners' sugar**
- 2 **cups flour**
- ¼ **teaspoon salt**

FILLING:
- ½ **cup almond paste, crumbled**
- 6 **ounces cream cheese**
- 2 **eggs**
- 1 **cup seedless raspberry preserves**

1. Preheat oven to 350° (375° at 6000'). For crust, beat butter and sugar until creamy. Add flour and salt. Blend just until a crumbly dough forms. Press onto the bottom of an ungreased 13" x 9" x 2" baking pan, building up the sides slightly. Bake 15-20 minutes, or until lightly browned. Cool on a rack 15 minutes.

2. For filling, beat almond paste with cream cheese until cream cheese is smooth. Add eggs, one at a time, beating lightly after each addition, until mixture is creamy. Spread evenly over baked crust.

3. Beat preserves to loosen consistency. Drizzle over filling in a random pattern, leaving some white spaces (some of the preserves will run under the cream cheese mixture). Bake in the center of oven 25-30 minutes, until cream cheese filling has set. Cool on a rack. Cut into bars or squares to serve.

12-15 servings

NOTE: To present as a tart, bake in an 11" tart pan with removable sides.

German Apple Cheesecake Bars

They will consider you a baking genius when you present these for dessert.

CRUST:
- 1 cup cold butter, cut into 16 pieces
- 2 cups flour
- ½ cup sugar
- ⅛ teaspoon salt

FILLING:
- 8 ounces cream cheese
- ½ cup sugar
- 1 egg
- ½ teaspoon vanilla extract
- 3 small tart apples, unpeeled and thinly sliced
  Cinnamon sugar (1 tablespoon ground cinnamon mixed with ½ cup sugar)

1. Preheat oven to 375° (400° at 6000′). For crust, cut butter into dry ingredients until mixture resembles coarse meal. Press into an 11″ x 9″ baking pan. Crust will be thick. Bake 15 minutes, or until lightly browned. Place on a rack. Reduce oven temperature to 350° (375° at 6000′).

2. For filling, beat cream cheese and sugar until smooth. Mix in egg and vanilla. Pour on top of crust.

3. Choosing the most uniform slices, arrange apple slices, edges touching, in matched parallel rows on the surface of the cream cheese mixture. (Apple slices will shrink a bit in baking.) Sprinkle with cinnamon sugar to taste, reserving the rest for another use. Bake 30 minutes, or until filling has set. Cool on a rack. Cut into bars, using apple slices as a guide.

12 servings

Sage Grouse

DREAM NIBBLERS

The name says it all! The ultimate chocolate bar!

BROWNIE CAKE:
- 4 ounces semi-sweet chocolate
- 1 cup butter
- 1½ cups sugar
- 4 eggs, beaten to blend
- 1 teaspoon vanilla extract
- 1 cup flour
- 1 cup chopped toasted pecans or walnuts

FILLING:
- 8 ounces cream cheese
- ⅓ cup sugar
- 1 egg
- 1 cup (6 ounces) semi-sweet chocolate chips

1. Melt chocolate and butter together in a large heavy saucepan over low heat. Remove from heat. Stir in sugar. Gradually blend in eggs and vanilla. Sift flour over batter in 2 additions, gently blending into batter after each addition. Do not beat. Gently stir in pecans. Pour into a buttered 13" x 9" x 2" baking pan. Set aside while preparing filling.

2. Preheat oven to 350° (375° at 6000'). For filling, beat together cream cheese and sugar until smooth. Beat in egg just until blended. Stir in chocolate chips. Drop large dollops of mixture randomly over the surface of chocolate batter. Swirl slightly with the flat side of a table knife to create a marbelized effect.

3. Bake in the center of oven 45 minutes, or until a toothpick inserted in the center of cake comes out just clean. Do not overbake. Cake should be moist like brownies. Cool on a rack.

16 servings

SIMPLE SESAMES

You will be saying, "Open sesame," all too often to your cookie jar when you make a batch of these easy refrigerator cookies.

   2 **cups butter**
1½ **cups sugar**
   3 **cups flour**
   1 **cup sesame seeds**
   2 **cups shredded coconut**
  ½ **cup chopped toasted almonds (blanched or unblanched)**

   1. Cream butter until smooth. Gradually beat in sugar until mixture is light and fluffy. Blend in flour. Mix in sesame seeds, coconut and almonds.
   2. Divide dough into thirds. Roll each third into a log 2 inches in diameter on a long sheet of waxed paper. Wrap tightly and refrigerate until firm (or freeze for use later).
   3. Preheat oven to 300° (325° at 6000'). Cut rolls into ¼" slices. Bake, 1" apart, on ungreased cookie sheets in the center of oven 20-25 minutes, until lightly browned. Cool on wire racks.

approximately 48 cookies

NOTE: Recipe may be halved.

Beginner's Luck

ORANGE FROSTED ORANGE COOKIES

These are soft, cake-like little mouthfuls that appeal to kids and grown-ups alike.

    3 cups flour
 1½ teaspoons baking powder
    ¼ teaspoon salt
    ½ teaspoon baking soda
    ½ cup buttermilk or sour milk
    ¾ cup butter
 1½ cups firmly packed light brown sugar
    2 eggs
    1 teaspoon vanilla extract
 1½ teaspoons grated orange rind
    ¾ cup chopped toasted pecans or walnuts

FROSTING:
    1 tablespoon butter
    2 cups confectioners' sugar
 1½ teaspoons grated orange rind
    ¼ cup orange juice (approximately)

1. Preheat oven to 350° (375° at 6000'). Stir together flour, baking powder and salt. Set aside. Dissolve baking soda in buttermilk. Set aside.

2. Cream butter and brown sugar until light and fluffy. Beat in eggs, one at a time. Add vanilla extract and orange rind. Blend in buttermilk mixture. Gently blend in flour mixture just until incorporated. Blend in nuts. Drop by teaspoonfuls, 2" apart, on greased cookie sheets. Bake 10-12 minutes, until lightly browned around the edges. Place on wire racks to cool.

3. For frosting, cream butter, confectioners' sugar and orange rind until smooth. Add enough orange juice to form a spreadable frosting that will not run off the cookies. Frost cookies when lukewarm.

approximately 48 cookies

TURTLE COOKIES

These easy-to-make cookies will remind you of a famous confection. They would attract attention at a bake sale, if you could get them past your family.

CRUST:
- 2 cups flour
- 1 cup firmly packed light brown sugar
- ½ cup butter
- ⅛ teaspoon salt
- 1 cup lightly toasted pecan halves

TOPPING:
- ⅔ cup butter
- ½ cup firmly packed light brown sugar
- 1 cup semi-sweet or milk chocolate chips

1. For crust, place flour, brown sugar and butter in a mixing bowl. With an electric mixer, blend ingredients until mixture resembles coarse meal. Press onto the bottom of a 13″ x 9″ x 2″ baking pan, making a slight rim. Scatter pecans over crust.

2. Preheat oven to 350° (375° at 6000′). For topping, melt butter with sugar in a heavy 2-quart saucepan, stirring until sugar dissolves. Bring mixture to a full boil, then cook 30 seconds. Pour evenly over pecans. Bake in the center of oven 18-20 minutes, or until golden brown. Place on a rack. Immediately sprinkle surface with chocolate chips. Allow to melt slightly (about 2 minutes), then swirl chips lightly to create a marbled effect. Cool completely before cutting into squares.

36-48 cookies

Wild Grasses

SCOTTISH SHORTBREAD

This is the ultimate butter cookie, straight from Scotland; so be sure to use the best tasting butter available.

   1 **cup butter**
   ½ **cup sugar**
   1½ **cups plus 2 tablespoons flour**
   ¾ **cup cornstarch**
   ⅛ **teaspoon salt**

1. Cream butter until smooth. Gradually add sugar, beating until mixture is light and fluffy. Gradually beat in flour, cornstarch and salt. Continue beating until a table knife will pull through dough cleanly. A small piece of dough held lightly between two fingers should not be sticky.

2. Preheat oven to 300°. Pat or spread dough smoothly in an ungreased 9" x 9" x 2" baking pan. Slice dough into 1¼" squares (or other desired shape). Prick each square 3 times with a fork, through to the bottom of dough. Bake in the center of oven about 1½-1¾ hours, until shortbread is faintly colored on the surface and golden on the bottom (cut a square out and look). Place pan on a rack. Immediately slice through original lines. Let cool completely before removing shortbread from pan.

approximately 48 cookies

NOTE: Recipe may be doubled or tripled.

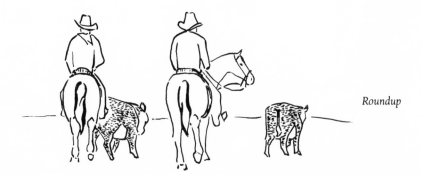

Roundup

RUSSIAN CREAM

A light and alluring dessert, perfect after a heavy meal.

1 **envelope unflavored gelatin**
¼ **cup cold water**
¾ **cup boiling water**
¾ **cup sugar**
1 **cup cold whipping cream**
1 **teaspoon vanilla extract**
1 **cup sour cream**

SAUCE:
1 **package (10 ounces) frozen strawberries in syrup, defrosted**
1 **package (10 ounces) frozen raspberries in syrup, defrosted**

Fresh berries and mint leaves (optional)

1. Sprinkle gelatin over ¼ cup cold water in a small saucepan and let soften for 5 minutes. Heat mixture slowly, stirring to dissolve gelatin. Combine with ¾ cup boiling water in a mixing bowl. Add sugar and stir until dissolved. Stir in cream and vanilla. Whisk sour cream to loosen its consistency. Add to gelatin mixture, whisking until mixture is smooth. Pour into a 1-quart ring mold, standard loaf pan or other mold. Chill several hours, until set.
2. To unmold, run a knife around edge of mold. Dip bottom of mold in hot water for 4-5 seconds. Dry mold. Center a serving plate upside down over mold. Holding both, invert. Remove mold. Decorate dessert with fresh berries and mint leaves, if desired.
3. Combine defrosted berries in a bowl and serve as a sauce. Alternatively, lightly sweetened fresh berries may be served with the Russian Cream.

8 servings

VARIATIONS: Substitute ¼-½ cup Amaretto or Grand Marnier for part of the ¾ cup boiling water (do not heat liqueur). Reduce sugar by 2-4 tablespoons.

Russian Cream may be served spooned from a bowl without being unmolded.

MOUSSE AU CHOCOLAT

Chocolate mousse may not be new, but the flavor and texture of this one are exquisite.

4 eggs, separated
2 tablespoons sugar
Pinch of salt
2 tablespoons cognac or Grand Marnier (or other liqueur)
6 ounces semi-sweet chocolate, cut into small chunks
3 tablespoons strong coffee
¼ cup butter, cut into 4 pieces

½ cup cold whipping cream

1. In a small, deep bowl, beat egg yolks until they start to thicken. Gradually add sugar, along with a pinch of salt, and beat until mixture is as thick and creamy as mayonnaise. Beat in the cognac.

2. Meanwhile, melt chocolate with coffee in a double boiler or heavy saucepan over low heat, stirring to blend ingredients. Remove pan from heat and stir in butter, one piece at a time, to form a smooth cream. Cool 5 minutes. Gradually add chocolate mixture to egg yolk mixture, beating until mixture is very thick and creamy.

3. Beat egg whites with a pinch of salt until stiff, but not dry. Stir about ¼ of the egg whites into the chocolate mixture to loosen it. Gently fold in the remaining egg whites. Gently scrape the mousse into a serving dish. Chill several hours, until set.

4. Before serving, whip cream. Decorate mousse with whipped cream piped through a pastry tube fitted with a star tip. Alternatively, serve whipped cream on the side.

8 servings

Moose in Winter

INDEX

This index is arranged in categories commonly used when planning cooperative entertaining events.

JACKSON HOLE A LA CARTE

A gift that can be opened again and again!

All proceeds from the sale of cookbooks go to support the efforts of the Jackson Hole Alliance, which works to protect the scenic, wildlife, and recreational resources of Jackson Hole.

To order by telephone, please call 1-307-733-9417

JACKSON HOLE ALLIANCE FOR RESPONSIBLE PLANNING
Post Office Box 2728, Jackson, Wyoming 83001

Please send _____ copies of **JACKSON HOLE A LA CARTE** $9.95 each $ _____

Postage and handling 1.60 each _____

Additional book mailed to same address 1.00 each _____

Wyoming residents add 4% sales tax per book .40 each _____

TOTAL $ _____

☐ Check enclosed. (Please make payable to the Jackson Hole Alliance).

☐ Bill my Mastercard   ☐ Bill my VISA

Card # _____ Expiration Date _____

Signature _____ Telephone (_____)_____

Please print
Name _____

Street or Box Number _____

City _____ State _____ Zip _____

JACKSON HOLE ALLIANCE FOR RESPONSIBLE PLANNING
Post Office Box 2728, Jackson, Wyoming 83001

Please send _____ copies of **JACKSON HOLE A LA CARTE** $9.95 each $ _____

Postage and handling 1.60 each _____

Additional book mailed to same address 1.00 each _____

Wyoming residents add 4% sales tax per book .40 each _____

TOTAL $ _____

☐ Check enclosed. (Please make payable to the Jackson Hole Alliance).

☐ Bill my Mastercard   ☐ Bill my VISA

Card # _____ Expiration Date _____

Signature _____ Telephone (_____)_____

Please print
Name _____

Street or Box Number _____

City _____ State _____ Zip _____